Soul of a Black Cop

James Booth,
Thanks for your
support. God bless!

Cover: Photograph by Brian Willingham
Design by Ebony Watkins
Inside photo of author by Judith Karns

Soul of a Black Cop

Second Edition

ISBN: 0-9785912-0-8

Soul of a Black Cop

BY BRIAN WILLINGHAM

Urban Humanities Publishing
A division of Willingham Enterprises
Flint, MI USA

Also by Brian Willingham

2003
Thunder Enlightening
The poetry and photography of a Black man in middle America

Thanks to Judith Karns, my editor, whose unwavering support and skill again transformed the echoes of my soul into the pages of a book. To Rhonda, my wife, sister, lover, friend and fellow artist, who not only supports but understands and shares my artistic ambition. To my mother, and black mothers across the planet, whose survival instinct is the foundation of black culture. To my children who are a daily reminder of the future and that the sky should always be the limit. Also a special thanks to Florence Dyer for the revisions, owner of Flo's Productions, visit online at www.flosproductions.biz. To the following scholars who took the time to evaluate and comment on my work: Herbert J. Gans, I. M. Gant, Maria Haberfeld, Sylvester Jones Jr., Leon F. Litwack, Kenneth J. Litwin, Marc Zimmerman , Howard Zinn and the afterword by Rev. Dr. James H. Cone.

Contents

Contents (continued)

A Word from the Editor

It is my hope that this book finds its way into the hearts and understanding of this nation's white readers. If this white publisher has learned nothing else from my association with my dear friend Brian Willingham, I have learned that racism still rages in our country, and inner-city Flint, Michigan, is an inescapable vortex, one of many microcosms of proof. Indeed, the incidents and the people in this book would not exist without racism, which comes in three forms: subtle, blatant and denied. This is not a story about a third-world country. It is our country. Human beings of any color conform to their cultural freedoms or lack thereof. The people and the lives to which you are about to be witness, the people the author serves every day, have nowhere else to go, and indeed, in their hopelessness and entrapment, cannot conceive of life as most of us live it.

-Judith Karns

Foreword

If you are reading this foreword, you are undoubtedly considering whether to take a guided tour through inner-city America with Police Officer Brian Willingham. As someone who has read *Soul of A Black Cop*, I advise you to leave your expectations behind, open your mind to a different interpretation than you are probably used to, open your eyes wide and look. The streetlights are not working; the urban landscape is dark with poverty and despair. Husbands beat their wives, children rob their neighbors, mothers smoke crack and sell their bodies to buy cheap gin. Teenagers murder their elementary school playmates in neighborhoods rotting from neglect.

Officer Willingham constructs a collage of daily misery for the uninitiated of us who are removed from the skeletal remains of once proud urban industrial mid-America. We, the readers, ride along on daily calls, listen to the stories given by offenders and victims, often unable to distinguish between the two, and witness how unemployment and the lack of social entitlements have turned the urban poor into ghosts walking down Martin Luther King Boulevard in search of a something seemingly unattainable.

In the course of his occupation, Officer Willingham participates in the daily lives of those at the margins of society, and contemplates reasons for the senseless behavior he encounters. However, rather than accepting facile logic and simply blaming the people he encounters for their deviant and criminal behavior, he insightfully focuses on pervasive unemployment and the lack of an effective public policy as major contributors to urban deterioration. *Soul of A Black Cop* is an effective indictment of the social system's inability to address the problems of the poor, the infirm and the abused through current law enforcement strategies.

With Officer Willingham as our daily guide and translator, we witness how the death of industrial production and the parallel governmental retreat from providing social entitlements to citizens has culminated in a culture of abuse; self-destruction has emerged as a festering blight. Drugs and alcohol calm the unquiet, while guns restore a sense of lost social power to powerless black men and boys. Black men go to prison, black women despair at their plight and black children raise themselves and other children all too often by relying on consumerist cultural images of misogyny and machismo promoted by the mainstream hip-hop culture.

Reflecting on his life in relation to the many destitute and humiliated people he encounters, Officer Willingham promotes an empathetic and a compassionate world view rather than the cold disdain for the poor all too frequently found in popular discourse. He always links individual behavior with structural and cultural forces and realizes that the problems encountered by most people existed long before they were born. He displays emotion too often missing from our "scientific" analyses of poverty and criminal behavior. While arresting a mother with hungry children he realizes the humiliation she must feel. He cries with joy for a family that discovers that a missing relative is alive.

Police officers go to places where most of us never go and see a part of our society that most of us bypass and pretend doesn't exist. However, while many police officers become jaded and treat citizens as objects to be acted upon with all the power and authority vested in the police role, Officer Willingham implores police officers to try and better the lives of people they make contact with. He is a different type of police officer from what most of us are used to seeing on television and in the movies. Rather than rejoicing over the arrest of "bad boys," he laments his inability to save people as probably the most painful experience he endures.

As a black police officer, Officer Willingham offers a unique view of his and other black officers' roles in society while avoiding simplistic reasoning often found in scientific journals. Black police officers were hired, in part, based on their assumed ability to interact better with members of African-American communities and reduce animosity between black citizens and police agencies. However, Officer Willingham shows us how the destruction of communities by structural and cultural forces over the last three decades has created a generational impasse between younger and older black men, which makes understanding and communication nearly impossible. Despite his empathy and desire for long-term solutions to social problems, his daily occupational life requires solving problems for the moment; he is asked to place his proverbial thumb in the dike of inhumanity and hold back the waves of despair from washing over the uninitiated.

Don't be too scared. Officer Willingham also acknowledges that feelings of fear and uncertainty swirl inside him. He too realizes that misery may appear to be destiny and the broken lives of most black people may never be repaired. However, his exploration is a form of catharsis and demands action. By forcing us to examine ourselves in relation to the lives of those we ignore or vilify, Officer Willingham teaches us that we can become more human. He demonstrates that by showing more concern for others we may become better human beings. His work is filled with hope and signs from above that emphasize resilience and the human ability to recover from impossible treatment.

Remaining blind is not an option for those who read this book. Officer Willingham chides us that we see without seeing and offers to serve as our guide to a world we know exists but choose to ignore. Rather than waiting until it is too late and comforting ourselves with, "I should have answered my brother's call," he demands that we become involved and work for social justice. Brian Willingham has a compelling story to tell. Are you curious? Okay. Process the emotion. You may feel faint. Fight back tears. Prepare for the next call on the tour and try to make sense of the senseless.

Kenneth Bolton Jr., Ph.D.
Co-author: *Black in Blue*
Associate Professor
Graduate Program Coordinator
Department of Sociology & Criminal Justice
Southeastern Louisiana University

Prologue

In April 2002, I received a two-week advanced notice of layoff from my duties as a police officer in Flint, Michigan. It was not a surprise. Talks of layoffs had dominated the conversations of police officers and other city employees. The tension surrounding layoffs was fueled by the fact that the city was nearly $30 million in debt, all of this on the heels of the 9/11 tragedy, which had its own negative economic effect on cities across America.

My city, where I was born and where I work, was embroiled in a bitter, racially divisive recall of a black male mayor. Other members of the Society of African-American Police and I had held a press conference in support of the black mayor, who eventually lost the recall election. In the midst of the political, racial and economic turmoil, the state of Michigan assumed receivership of Flint, which meant that Flint citizens or its elected officials no longer had control of our city government. City council members would spend $250,000 of taxpayer money fighting the state's decision, only to lose, yet the council members would complain that they could not afford to pick up trash from streets of Flint's poorest black neighborhoods. When I patrolled these areas, I would see discarded appliances, automobile parts and other debris that in some cases partially blocked streets.

People who live there would tell me their calls to local representatives went unanswered. City government had forgotten these places. I saw that race and politics paid a huge role in how people are served by the system.

At the time, I wrote a weekly column in a local black newspaper. I took pictures of the debris and wrote about it. I received an angry phone call from the ward councilman. A day later, the councilman held a press conference at the site of the debris as he had it cleared away. Subsequently, the councilman placed permanent roadblocks in the area, which prevented any further illegal dumping.

The city prepared to eliminate 36 police positions in the face of a recently renewed millage to retain 40 police positions. Too, I knew that in recent years, city council members and many city department heads had improved their pay and benefits.

Before my layoff, I had been asked by my union to help campaign for the renewal of the millage with the understanding that it would prevent others and me from being laid off. I walked neighborhoods, planted yard signs, attended meetings, organized events, and spoke publicly to the media in favor of the millage.

Following my layoff, I addressed the city council as a new civilian and asked about the millage money and how it affected the decision to lay off police officers. I questioned why the community was asked to renew the millage in the name of saving 40 positions, only to see 36 positions eliminated. I asked: "Where is the millage money? Is it in a separate fund? Has it been intermingled with the general fund?" I got no answers, and as I spoke, a police union leader left the meeting with a disgusted look on his face, I assume not happy with my inquiry.

I wondered why the police union hadn't questioned the city council about the millage money, but I decided that it was not worth the time and effort to further explore something no one else seemed to care about. I have learned that no amount of fighting and resisting change can circumvent certain problems.

White officers had approached me in the past and said, "Why do we need black police organizations? We should all be blue," suggesting that officers of all colors were treated the same, and were viewed the same.

Of course, this isn't true, as unresolved disparaties can be found across the board in black and white promotions, assignments and discipline.

Black police officers found their names written on the walls in the police department: *Black mayor, you can go, and on your way out, take the black police officers' organization, Willingham and (so and so, and so and so) with you!*

As I continued to patrol the streets during the first of the two weeks before my layoff, I was depressed at the thought of trying to solve people's problems while risking my life, when my own future was uncertain. When I wear a uniform, badge, bullet proof vest, and carry a gun, I must be mentally and physically prepared to take on whatever challenge may be presented in the line of duty. I realized very quickly that, because of the fact of my imminent layoff, I was not prepared, nor was I willing to assume this duty. I wondered how any city government could expect a police officer to successfully perform knowing that he soon won't have a job. I believe it should be policy that a soon-to-be-laid-off police officer should never take the to the streets. In the final week of my layoff notice, I took a series of sick and vacation days to keep myself off the streets.

When I became a police officer, I had concerns about having a gun in the house because I have three small children. Never in my life had I owned a gun. Now it became normal to have a gun in my home. I remember the first time my children saw me in my police uniform during my academy graduation. They ran to me and hugged me after the ceremony. My mother cried and my wife smiled as they looked on. A particular pride and honor is bestowed upon a police officer and his family, especially in the beginning of a career. However, by the time I received a layoff notice more than four years later, all the new paraphernalia associated with policing was old news in my family.

On my last day, I packed my police gear in the same old Army duffel bag I used to bring it home years back. At the station, I met with the quartermaster.

"Damn, you comin' to bring that stuff in now?" he said. "They were supposed to tell you guys to make appointments. Hell, I haven't even had lunch. I'm starved."

"Well, you know how it is around here," I said. "Nobody told me anything. I can come back if you want me to."

"Naw, I'll go ahead and take care of you since you're already here, but I'm sick of this place. I just took over this job and shit was all fucked up down here. Every time you turn around somebody's pickin' up shit or turnin' in shit. I wish the city would make up its mind."

Since I was the one losing the job, I found his attitude insensitive, but I tried to understand it. The man was only in his 40s, but he had already suffered a heart attack from work-related stress. Besides, it was true, officers were constantly being laid off and called back to work, some as many as four times. It got to a point where some officers took jobs in more stable communities, while others who had not yet been laid off started jumping ship to other departments. When he was done bitching, we started the inventory.

"Four pairs of pants," he said.

"Got it."

"Three long sleeve shirts. Three short sleeve."

"Right here."

"Gun."

I laid my 9mm handgun on the table with the slide cocked to the rear, together with five fully loaded clips. He checked the serial number and it didn't match up. We discovered that my partner and I had mistakenly switched guns. I recalled that during the last arrest my partner and I made, we locked our guns in the same compartment near the elevator before transporting a prisoner up to the booking area. Guns are not allowed in prisoner booking areas. Evidently, after the arrest, we both grabbed the wrong hardware and never noticed it. If either of us had shot anyone in the line of duty with the wrong gun, we would have had hell explaining it. I called my partner right away. He rushed to the station and we straightened things out. I was embarrassed, but the quartermaster handled it without notifying supervision. I appreciated that. Then we continued the inventory.

"Got your badge and police ID?"

"Right there on the table."

Shortly after that, the phone rang and the quartermaster walked away to answer it. I stared at my badge lying on that table. I felt an impulse to put it in my pocket. Maybe he wouldn't notice when he returned. I looked at my police identification and couldn't help but think that I had literally turned in my identity.

After nearly five years of police work, I had adjusted. That adjustment also meant that I had learned to suppress feelings. I walked out of the room casually, with that empty duffel bag, as if leaving behind a huge part of me didn't matter. The truth was eating away at me in about the same manner as my first homicide did. Once I reached the hallway, I saw other officers in uniform. They all wished me good luck, but they seemed preoccupied with police business. There were no long heartfelt good-byes. This was the very nature of policing. I continued walking with that duffel bag flung over my shoulder as if it didn't bother me. Immediately, I had become an outsider to the culture. In that instant, I was no longer who I thought I was.

Before this, my children had begun to complain that their school friends asked too many questions about what it was like to have a police officer for a father. After my layoff, my kids didn't ask many questions about police work. All they cared about was that I was home every day to spend time with them. Many months went by before they began to wonder why I didn't go to work anymore.

"I'm laid off honey," I responded to the first question.

"What does laid off mean? Is that like being fired?"

"No sweetie, it's not like being fired. Well, sort of. I didn't do anything wrong. It just means that the city doesn't have enough money to pay everyone, so they tell some people they can't work anymore."

"Well, why did they pick you? Is that fair?"

"Because I'm one of the newest people. Those who have worked the longest get to stay. That's fair, I think."

"Hmm, so you're not a police officer anymore, Daddy?"

"No, not for now."

"So you don't have to go to work?"

"No, not for now."

"So you get to stay home with us?"

"Yes, for now."

"Yea, Daddy gets to stay home with us," the three of them yell.

Finally, my daughter sums up the conversation: "Can we go to the beach?"

The experience taught me that kids do not care what their parents do for a living or if they work at all. What they care about most is how much time their parents spend with them.

I spent the summer on the beach with my children discovering who I was minus the badge and gun. I wrote the bulk of my first book, *Thunder Enlightening, The poetry and photography of a Black man in middle America*, during that time.

In November 2002, I was called back to work, ending some uncertainties in my life. The same night I was called back, two police officers from my department died in a hunting accident. As I stood in a city administrative office the following morning completing papers to return, I could hear workers casually stating that the death of the two officers meant that two additional officers on layoff could be called back. To some, this is all their deaths meant. I was glad to be back, yet, I was sad to see that in police culture, nobody misses you when you're gone.

As I am soon to discover, things never change, and things will never be the same.

ONE

The Mourning After

TWO NAMELESS, faceless young black males are victims of a drive-by shooting. The life of one young man in particular takes shape for me because I cross paths with his frantic mother.

She approaches me just as I tie the infamous yellow crime scene tape to a telephone pole at a city street corner. We stand together in front of a dilapidated green house. The bodies of two young black men are lying on the ground behind the house. Word spreads quickly through the "hood" that one of those apparently lifeless bodies is that of her son. Though I don't yet have names, other officers at the scene tell me that at least one of the men is already dead. One man is 21 and the other is 17. That's all I know, and that can seem cold and callous to the frantic mother who just wants to confirm whether or not her child is living. She desperately presses me for more information, making me feel as if I am conspiring to worsen her suffering.

From where the mother and I stand, we can see the legs of one man. Like so many young black men who have been killed on the streets of Flint, Michigan, the grass in the yard at this death scene has also been killed. It has been so neglected that dirt surrounds the paint chipped house on all sides. The house next door only adds to the feeling of loss. It has been abandoned and tall weeds grow around it. The unusually cool August sun is setting and it illuminates dust clouds that hover just above the bodies that lie on the ground.

By now, a large crowd of people fill the intersection behind the mother and me to watch paramedics straddle the body of one man. This causes the dust clouds, and hope, to stir just a little. Little wind is blowing and things seemed to stand still as the paramedics pump the man's chest.

I restrain the frantic mother as she tells me her son's name. Not knowing what else to do, I asked her the usual follow-up questions that no doubt seem stupid, when her child may be dead or dying as I speak. She is so overwhelmed with grief that she can hardly spell her child's name, or recall addresses and phone numbers. Finally, I learn that his name starts with a *D* and that he is either 21 or 22 years old. I know he is the one thought to be dead at the scene, but I cannot tell her this. Therefore, I watch her cling to a false hope that I know will eventually fail her. It is difficult to watch someone hope, wish and pray for a dead loved one to live. As I listen to her prayers, I know God has already spoken.

At the scene, my duties call for me to deny what seems to be the most humane thing a person can do at a death scene. That is to confirm whether or not her child is dead, alive, or even a victim of the seemingly endless brutal violence that has become America's black urban community.

"Just let me go see," she says repeatedly.

"Hey, man, that's her son lying over there; she can't go see him?" someone else yells angrily out of the crowd at me.

"Is that him? I can't tell," she says to a young black man after looking toward the bodies.

"Yeah, that's him, I know it's him, I already know it's him," the man replies to her with a brutal yet caring honesty. I can feel the intensity of the mother's grief in the tightness of her hands as they grip mine. I feel her body shivering. I see the anguish on her face. I then motion for the young man to console the mother, something I would like to do, and he steps in, hugs the mother, and gently pulls her a couple feet away from the tape.

I think at that moment that no American struggles more than the black woman who has raised children with little or no help from the father, only to see their lifeless bodies loaded into an ambulance. The one thing I have never seen is a black father grieving the death of a child at one of these scenes. I can't help but think that if more black men had loving relationships with their children, less black-on-black crime would happen.

It is the black mother who sits on the front line of the birth and murder of her sons. She follows the ambulance containing her son's body, possibly to the hospital where he was born. She waits impatiently for news of his status just as she did when he was born. The body makes a brief stop in the trauma unit, where some doctor will officially pronounce it dead. Finally, she is asked to identify his body in a morgue. The hospital is the first place that she ever laid eyes on his tiny body wrapped in a blanket. It is where she first supported his head, smelled his skin, rubbed his hair and counted his fingers and toes. It was where she first proudly gave strangers the correct spelling of his name for his birth certificate. Now she must do the same for his death certificate.

The social system that produces death in poor black communities seems more fascinated with trying to revive dead black bodies than eliminating the suffering that causes death. The urgency on the part of the system to save black people has more to do with the image of the system than the welfare of the people. We have reached a point in American life where police, paramedics, and those citizens who stand and watch are no longer surprised or appalled by the deaths of young black men, which deaths have become a normal occurrence for everyone except the black mother. She is the only person left on the planet who openly grieves the loss of her sons as abnormal.

My job is to insure that no one contaminates the crime scene in a community already contaminated with unemployment, drugs, poor housing and declining schools. The contamination is evident in the lives of the many who stand at the street corner as the paramedics move bodies, and the news media stands at a distance filming the horror for the nightly news. The sentiments of those tuning in for the night's top story and those buying the following day's newspaper would more than likely be the same as the sentiments of those who stand on the corner: "Just another nigga dead man, just another nigga dead; don't nobody care."

Just a few blocks away shots are fired into the air, but nobody reacts with surprise or fear. In this neighborhood the shots are just a sign of frustration, acknowledgment that another soldier has been killed, and probably a sign that justice will be served one way or another.

Finally they load the bodies onto stretchers and begin carrying them to the ambulances parked on the street not far from the yard. During the short journey, the victims' limbs dangle awkwardly from the edges of the stretchers.

For a desperate mother, any movement from their bodies is perhaps falsely perceived as a sign of life rather than death.

After paramedics remove the victims, I move closer to the crowd.

"Did anybody see anything?" I ask.

"Did the police see anything?" a young black male member of the crowd sarcastically fires back. "There was two unmarked cars sitting down the street when the shooting happened, and they took off and went the other way."

I sympathize with the people who stand on the corners that I once walked, on which I played and rode my bike long before General Motors eliminated 80,000 jobs and crack cocaine came to stay. I was here before the schools began to fail and so many houses became vacant and boarded up. I sympathize because political leaders are constantly stating that the poor economy is a national problem, yet only the landscape of the black community has changed so drastically since the late 1970s.

I sympathize with the people on the corner, because they are right. "Just another nigga' dead, nobody cares."

In fact, society has come to expect that black people will undoubtedly continue to effortlessly destroy themselves. The problem belongs to blacks and blacks alone. Nobody believes that it can or will end, therefore serious solutions are not sought. This in turn suggests that society is satisfied, maybe even happy that so many black men are dying so young. The survivors standing at homicide scenes sense that black life does not hold the same value as white life. For them, the reality contaminates the daily events that make up their lives and renders them numb and emotionless during their most tragic moments.

In this crowd, I see many familiar faces of young adults whom I have known as students in Flint schools. They have traded childhood innocence for the bitter reality that lies before them on the ground. Among those people stands a beautiful young pregnant woman I recognize. I find the irony of one mother carrying a child and another mourning the death of a child on the same corner both emotionally and spiritually moving. I wonder if this is but an odd rite of passage for the black circle of life. How might the fate of the expectant mother and her unborn child be connected to this moment? She doesn't cry, but she does watch the grieving mother. The grieving mother hasn't forgotten how to mourn. She cries for all who no longer remember.

TWO

No Peace of Mind

ON OUR final call of the night, my partner and I are dispatched to a shooting. Upon arrival, I speak to a black woman who states that she heard two or three shots on the east side of her house near the driveway. She then heard a loud banging noise at the side door. When she went to the door, she found a young black man, 19 years old, who had been shot. She knows him. She let him inside and told him to lie down on the kitchen floor on his back as she called 9-1-1.

The man has been shot in the chest one time with what seems to be a small caliber weapon. He states that he has asthma and is having trouble breathing. Though he gives the names of the young black men who shot him, he won't discuss the circumstances surrounding his being shot.

I sense he is being evasive about the details, but I give him the benefit of the doubt because paramedics are working on him. His medical care is more important than my questions, although I would like to have as much information as possible to solve the crime if he should die.

I ride with him in the ambulance, where paramedics state that his condition is worsening. When we arrive at the hospital, the man is rushed into the trauma room where medical professionals are already set up to treat him. Again, the need for me to get information from him is secondary to the job of nurses and doctors. I stand at a distance and gather as much information on his medical condition as I can.

I watch as they strip off his clothing. I watch as the doctors flip his naked body and check for wounds. He has one bullet wound—an entry in the upper back and an exit in the lower chest. He is still alert, yelling and screaming when he is touched and squeezed on his upper torso by doctors. After x-rays, he is prepped for emergency surgery where doctors will cut open his abdomen and check for internal damage. The doctor in charge states that he is in serious condition. He is whisked away to surgery. I don't get another chance to talk to him, but under the circumstances, the least I can report is that he was alert and conscious before surgery.

I speak to his mother briefly. From her I am able to get the proper spelling of her son's name, his date of birth, address, and phone number. She asks how her son is doing. Reminding her that I am not a qualified medical professional, I tell her that her son was alert when I saw him, and seemed OK. Another woman with her asks what my opinion of his medical condition is based upon what I saw, and I tell her again that he seems OK and reiterate that I am not qualified to give official medical information on his condition. Finally,

I am done with this case. I return to the station to leave a report.

Months later, I am subpoenaed to court on the case. A major snowstorm is coming. The activity at the courts is slow. The prosecutor is stuck in the storm and is running late. The detective in charge of the case informs me that the victim is also stranded at home without a ride. She doesn't seem to bothered by the fact that the victim may not make it to court, although the case would be lost without him. He is the best witness. He grew up with the young black man who shot him. They were friends.

I volunteer to pick him up. He lives across town in an apartment complex with his mother and younger siblings. When I pick him up, he tells me his not having a ride had more to do with his fear of retaliation from the suspect than anything else. He has received several threats warning him not to appear in court. Since the suspect is known to firebomb houses, the victim is even more concerned. He knows the police can't protect him outside the courtroom.

Successful prosecution of cases is a feather in the cap of police and prosecutors. However, what does it mean for the victims who are left to face family and friends of the criminals who seek revenge? Even I wanted to pick up the victim so that my good police work won't go to waste. It is just another case for me. However, until I talk to this young man personally, I don't fully comprehend that he is a human being who will still have to live after the case has been prosecuted.

I convince him that he must testify. During the ride, he tells me he has no money and no job, and that he and his family can't afford to move or run and hide. In addition, he is in pain because he can't afford to fill his prescription for pain medication. The bullet, which entered his back, just missed his spinal cord. During his emergency surgery his stomach had to be cut open. In all, the ride in the ambulance and total medical treatment left him with a bill of $9,000 that he can't pay.

When we arrive at the courts, I inform the detective and the prosecutor of his fears. They convince him that it is best for him to testify, and he does. Afterward he lies on a bench outside the courtroom complaining of stomach pain. At the end of the day, I escort him and his family outside to his uncle's car because they are afraid. When it is all said and done, I felt reasonably sure the suspect will make a plea agreement, which will mean a long prison sentence, but what will it mean for the victim? Will he receive justice and live happily ever after, or will he be living in a prison of sorts himself, not knowing when the enemy might strike again?

THREE

Survival

NEARLY HALFWAY through my shift this night, I am dispatched to a call to take a report for domestic violence. The victim is a white woman who is six months pregnant. The suspect, her boyfriend, is a black man. She has concerns that her baby may have been hurt when her boyfriend punched her in the stomach. She smokes a cigarette as she tells me about her concern for the well-being of her unborn child. With the cigarette hanging from her lips, bobbing up and down as she speaks through the corners of her mouth, she pulls up her shirt to show me bruises near her ribs and on her arms. I try to encourage her to meet me at the hospital so she can check the status of her baby and file a police report at the same time. She is very hesitant. She seems to want more sympathy than police protection. This suggests to me that she might not be all that serious about filing a complaint, and that she may have low self-esteem.

She goes into the house and takes her time coming out. She enters a van with another woman whom I assume is driving her to the hospital. I follow them a short distance and realize they are not going in the direction of the hospital. Giving her the benefit of the doubt, I go to the hospital, but she never arrives.

Just as I am about to leave the hospital, I receive a call from dispatch stating that an ambulance is en route to the hospital with a 4-year-old black boy who has been struck by a van while on his bicycle. I change emotional gears from just casually waiting at the nurses' station for the pregnant woman to file a report, to standing in a highly intense trauma situation in which doctors and staff prepare for the arrival of this child. My initial task is to report the child's condition as given to me by the doctor in charge.

Suddenly, paramedics rush him into the trauma room. The child has multiple fractures to the face and head, but he is still breathing. Doctors run tests to measure the rising pressure inside his skull. His pupils are fixed and dilated. His lungs are also badly bruised. His status is critical. His pulse is dropping rapidly. Doctors massage his heart, but that doesn't seem to make a difference. Amid the confusion, I begin to pray. I ask God to restore this child's pulse. Moments later his pulse does improve, but still, medically, it does not appear that he is going to live.

I am met in the trauma room by an African-American male chaplain who is about my age, 38. Together we talk to the family members, who by now have crowded a waiting room. They are awaiting news, but it is too soon to know anything except that the child is still living. Not one of the more than 20 family members is male. I try to talk to the mother, but she has gone into another consciousness. Her eyes are blank and glossy. She is talking to the child, though he is not in the room.

"When you wake up you will get your honeybun and juice," she repeats again and again.

I turn to the grandmother to get a name, date of birth, address and phone number. She is more stable but especially distraught because she had a dream the night before that another of her grandchildren was struck by a car. She states that usually she talks daily by telephone to the child who is now in critical condition. This day something prevented her from calling, so she partially blames herself for the accident.

I remain at the hospital until the end of my shift at midnight. I make a final check on the child before I leave and find that he is still living. However, he is still not out of the woods.

I do not sleep well on this night. I wake up several times throughout the night thinking of this child. Finally at about 8 a.m. I call the emergency room nurses' desk. I know they will not give certain information to just anyone over the phone, so I identify myself before asking questions. I am transferred to the pediatric intensive care unit where I am told that his condition still hasn't improved, but he is still living.

I am sad for this family, and I am honored that I am involved with their tragedy. Through this experience, I am reminded of the reason I became a police officer, and that was simply to help people. I feel a need to find a way to help this family. I wonder if I have done enough to inform children about safety in Flint. I contact the child's school and ask his classmates to draw pictures for him. I contact the Flint School's safety office and volunteer to do more safety presentations for elementary children.

I meet his mother and grandmother the following day and they are in better spirits. The mother tells me the child's jaw is broken in two places and he has blood in one of his lungs. They invite me to visit the child and walk me to his room. He doesn't look much better than the night before, but he seems stronger. He is breathing much easier. I encourage his mother to talk to him because I read somewhere that people in critical condition can still hear. She says she talks to him constantly. I think nothing can make a child heal better than the voice of his own mother.

Three months later, I am called to a particular street for domestic violence. The child and his mother live on the same street. After taking the report, I ask the victim if she is familiar with the incident and she informs me that the family lives just two doors from her. I make a surprise visit and find that the child is now walking, talking and eating crackers. After all of the trauma and multiple surgeries he endured, the only problem he now suffers is a slight loss of vision. What I find amazing is the ability of some human beings to survive what seem to be humanly impossible circumstances. It reminds me that this is what life is about for poor African Americans: survival.

FOUR

Six Hours of an Eight-Hour Shift

My PARTNER and I are dispatched to a grocery store where a black female shoplifter has become violent with store security. When we arrive, we find that the woman has three young daughters with her.

Security tells us the woman poured out 48 cans of beer throughout the store and attempted to refund the bottles to buy a 40-oz. bottle of beer and cigarettes. She gives us a false name, but we find her ID in her vehicle outside the store. Then we check her police records. She has six misdemeanor warrants and two felonies for various larcenies and frauds. We then add fresh charges of false information to police, retail fraud (shoplifting), and contributing to the delinquency of minors. Policy dictates that we impound her vehicle for safekeeping, otherwise we could be held responsible for any damages that might occur if we leave the car in the lot. We also find that the woman has driven without a license.

We find that she is unemployed and she and the children are basically homeless. They live in a rundown hotel. We transport the woman and her children to the station and I can hear the children's voices filtering through the Plexiglas partition from the back seat of our cruiser. They tell their mother they are hungry. She obviously has no power to feed them while being under arrest, but this doesn't matter to the hungry kids. For me, to be under arrest with hungry children would be a humiliating experience. I wondered how she is able to feed them even when she has her freedom. I wonder why she is not trying to steal food for her children instead of beer. It would make more sense and perhaps be more honorable, but by law, stealing is stealing. Under the circumstances, Children's Protective Services will need to be notified, which means that she might lose custody. If she is eventually lodged in jail on any of her warrants or fresh charges, we will have no choice but to place the children in emergency foster care.

When we reach the station, the already traumatized children become even more frantic when we separate them from their mother during the booking process. I sit with the children to try to calm them as my partner has their mother fingerprinted and photographed. The children cry constantly and ask many questions. Most of all, they want to know what is happening to their mother and if they are going to be taken away from her. I honestly cannot tell them what to expect. I don't want to see them taken from their mother, but I wonder if being with their mother is in their best interest.

After the children and I warm up to each other, they smile and play. I admire their resilience under the unique circumstances they face. Finally, the oldest girl, who sits between her younger sisters, raises her hand as if she is in a classroom and says to me in a particular voice, with a particular look on her face, "We hungry!" As a father of three children of nearly identical ages, I know the voice and the look very well. They just naturally assume I have the power to feed them. After all, I am a police officer. The public expects the police to be resourceful. In many cases, the expectation is unreasonable, but in this case I really can't imagine telling the children that feeding them doesn't fit into my job description. I ask them what they want to eat. They smile, look at each other quizzically, and wait for someone to speak up. When no one speaks right away, I walk away as if leaving, and I tell them I can't get them anything to eat if they don't know what they want. This is something I do with my own children when they won't decide. They quickly put their heads together, and before I get too far away the answer comes. "Pizza. We want pizza," the oldest one says.

I go to a local pizzeria and explain the situation. I ask for a pizza and drinks for the kids. I explain that I have no cash on me, and offer to pay for the pizza the following day. The manager of the pizza establishment shares that she had a similar childhood experience and gladly donates the items. By the time the children finish their food, their mother's processing is complete.

Because of budget cuts, the city jail is closed and the county jail will not lodge the woman for any of her warrants or fresh charges because they don't involve any serious injury to anyone. However, it is unknown what mental damage she has inflicted upon her children during the ordeal. The woman and her children are free to go. They have no transportation and are now stranded at the station. My partner and I drive them back to their hotel. Overall, we spend more than six hours of an eight-hour shift dealing with this family. I spend the remaining hour and a half of my shift working alone as my partner completes the report.

FIVE

Why am I here?

WHILE PATROLLING slowly on a cold November evening with my partner, I nearly strike a black woman who is walking in the middle of a dark side street. Because the city is in financial distress, many such streets in poor black communities are without working streetlights. A speeding driver could have killed her. The lack of streetlights is only part of the problem. It is as if she has a death wish, the way she continues to stroll so casually after turning her head and seeing us drive up behind her. Since she doesn't bother to get out of the street, we stop to talk to her. Everyone has a story, and I am curious.

She tells us she's in her 30s and has been on the streets since age 16. Street people are usually labeled as the most undesirable among society. She breaks the mold. She is easily the most beautiful woman I have ever seen walking the street. Her brown skin is smooth and without blemish. When she manages a smile, her white teeth seem perfect. On inspection, we find that her coat pockets contain a couple crack pipes, a cheap bottle of gin and more than $50 from "tricks" she has turned this night. As if it will save her, my partner throws the small glass pipes to the ground in disgust and crushes them beneath his feet. Then to further accent his purpose, he pours out the gin and launches the bottle into the nearby yard of a vacant home. He gives her the usual pep talk about the dangers of the streets. The pain and shame in her eyes are obvious. She tells us she has a 13-year-old whose birthday is tomorrow. She is working the streets to earn money to buy a gift for her. After my partner's speech, she flashes a pretty smile that contains a girlish innocence she probably had before she started working the streets.

We watch as she walks off in the distance, toward the one streetlight that is working at the corner of the next main street. Turning right, she walks out of sight. My partner and I get back in the cruiser and sit in silence for about five minutes. I know we are both thinking it is a shame that any life would be wasted on the streets, but the fact that this woman is so beautiful punctuates that shame even more. We both want to save her, and neither of us can. Our inability to save people is probably the most painful experience for police officers who care.

My perception of my role in policing is to better the lives of people with whom I come into contact. When I can't do that, I ask myself, "Why am I here?"

SIX

Thanksgiving Dinner

THE DAY before Thanksgiving on the final call of the night, my partner and I respond to an armed robbery in progress at a liquor store. Two men, one with a handgun, have entered the store and demanded money. Before we arrive, dispatch states that the armed man has climbed over the counter and shots are possibly being fired. The cashier, who is a black male, has escaped from the store and locked the robbers inside.

As we arrive on the scene, we find one of the suspects trying to kick open a steel door on the north side of the store. I draw my weapon and take cover behind a trash receptacle. I am watching the steel door move as if it might open with each kick by the suspect. I feel a tremendous amount of fear that if that door opens, I will need to make a split-second decision to shoot or not to shoot. Though I have good reason to believe the suspect is armed, I can't see through steel to verify this. The possibilities exist that I could shoot and kill an unarmed person or be killed by my own hesitation. I decide to shoot if that door opens. I even consider shooting through it before it opens, but that is an overreaction. So I wait.

I think daily about the possibility of using deadly force as a police officer. Sometimes I even have nightmares in which I am in shoot-outs with suspects. I often don't remember the nightmares. I am embarrassed sometimes by what my wife tells me I say in my sleep. Someone is usually trying to kill me or I am trying to kill someone. Subconsciously, I must have a fear of these things, because in real life I have never been shot at and I have only had to fire my weapon at vicious dogs.

My partner goes to the east door and through it he sees another suspect pacing through the store in a panic. I can hear my partner order the man to lie on the floor.

From my position, I am still watching the steel door move. Having more time to think, I am more confident about my decision to shoot.

Soon, an army of police officers from all over the county surrounds this tiny store in the middle of the black community. Now many more guns are drawn. The decision to shoot is not totally mine anymore and I am relieved. The store clerk returns with the key. A sergeant unlocks the door and storms inside with a team of officers. The men are arrested without incident and everyone goes home safe.

Facing high stress situations teaches police officers much about themselves. By the end of this call I learn that I really didn't want to kill anyone, even when I had the legal authority to do so. The responsibility of taking a human life is not something I think I can easily live with, though I accept it as a possibility.

I think about how on television and movies, the sight of a police officer taking cover in preparation for a shoot-out is highly glamorized. However, when I am behind a trash receptacle on Thanksgiving eve, kneeling in broken glass, surrounded by the smell of urine, I find nothing glamorous about it. All I want to do is make it home for Thanksgiving dinner.

SEVEN

No Support, No Control

ONE EVENING I receive a call to handle a domestic assault report. When I arrive, I meet a 19-year-old black girl who tells me her 12-year-old cousin has been physically abused by her mother. She tells me the mother has stomped her daughter in her chest and punched her in the head.

Finally, the mother intervenes and says she disciplined the child when she failed to clean her room as she was instructed. She adds that the child has been expelled from every school in the city. The mother states that she used a belt to discipline the child. When the child grabbed the belt and fell to the floor holding it, she placed her foot on the child to gain leverage so she could pull the belt away from her.

The mother is trying to keep control of her child. Many children are learning to use the system against their parents to avoid physical discipline. The mother and I are both in our late 30s, and we both acknowledge that we were raised on physical discipline. I explain to her that it is lawful to physically discipline a child as long as the discipline is reasonable, but the interpretation of "reasonable" by a government agency that doesn't understand black culture will handicap black parents. When children head down the wrong path, and they sense that their parents' hands may be tied, they can become even more rebellious. The same system that criticizes single black mothers for not controlling their children also punishes them for trying to establish control. Thus, a black parent with an at-risk child may be at a loss for a means to control the child. The government will, however, find a way to control children by placing them in juvenile homes, and eventually jails and prisons.

The mother explains how she has already become entangled in the system with an older daughter who she caught having sex in her home when she was 13. When she physically disciplined the daughter, the daughter went to school the following day and reported the mother to a teacher. In turn, the teacher informed Children's Protective Services. What followed was an investigation that resulted in the daughter being placed in foster care. Children's Protective Services then went to the schools of the mother's other three children and investigated them as well. The mother was given an ultimatum to get into counseling and parenting classes or risk losing all of her children. Eventually she got the oldest child back, but now the 12-year-old seems to be trying to send her through the process again. Though I wish the mother luck and urge her to continue fighting to save her child from the streets, I leave her knowing she has no clear-cut direction as to how she would accomplish the task, and neither do I.

EIGHT

Street-corner Judge and Jury

NEAR THE end of our shift this night, my partner and I stop a 37-year-old black woman who is driving at a high rate of speed in a residential area. She is intoxicated and does not have her license in possession.

After talking with her, we find that she is unemployed and raising three children alone. The children will not have Christmas this year because there is no money. We can impound her car and write her three tickets that she no doubt can't afford and probably will make no attempt to pay.

The most extreme action we can take would be to arrest the woman for drunk driving. Since it is a weekend and no courts are open, she likely would sit in county jail two or three days. Legally we could justify the most extreme action against her, but morally we agree to hold our own court at that intersection. We remind her that she could have died or killed someone else if we hadn't stopped her. Surely then this would have been a bad Christmas for her family. We encourage her to get help for her drinking. We can't be sure that any of the breaks we give her will actually help her, but neither can we be sure that throwing the book at her will remedy her problems.

I look at her in the back seat of our cruiser, and I can see the tears streaming down her face as we drive her home to her children. After we release the woman from the back of our cruiser, I watch her walk a lonely walk to the door of her home. We wait until she places the key in the door and opens it before we drive away. In a world conditioned to see material things as success, the mere physical presence of healthy family members may not seem like much. Yet, it is more than many people have. When I look at it that way, the woman's situation doesn't seem so bad.

NINE

Social Justice?

MY SHIFT is almost over when my partner and I are dispatched to a breaking and entering call. The location is near where I spent part of my childhood. I meet with the victim, a single black mother with three children, who is renting a small dilapidated home. Her 14-year-old daughter states that when she entered the side door alone she heard strange noises in the basement, at which time she yelled and ran from the house. Once outside the house, she watched two young black males run from the house. She knows them both.

I get a list of missing items and check the house to ensure no suspects remain. The house is poorly lit. I enter the side door and walk to the kitchen. Old food is on the table. The linoleum is peeling from the floor. Doors to the kitchen cabinets are either broken or missing. I continue to the living room where bags of clothing are strewn across the floor. The mother says she is preparing to move a few blocks away. The door to a back bedroom has been kicked at the hinges. I look inside the room and out the window and see an old rusted fire pit that has been placed beneath the window and used as a step by the child burglars.

After getting a list of missing items, I find one of the suspects who lives up the street. He is just 12 years old.

I explain to his mother that he was seen running from the house, and that I will be forced to arrest him. She cooperates. I take him to the station and book him. A sergeant talks to his mother and she refuses to grant him permission to question her son. It is nearly midnight. The sergeant orders me to contact the family court emergency system to see if they will lodge the 12-year-old in a detention center. When talking to the family court, I explain to them that I do not believe it would be necessary to lodge this child in a center. The mother knows there will be consequences if she doesn't have her son in court when she is ordered. He will still be brought to justice in time, but I feel that removing him from the home on this night will not make things any more just.

It won't change the fact that his mother is an unemployed drug user, raising six children alone. It won't change the fact that his father is in prison. It won't change the fact that the neighbor whose home he broke into is also a single mother of three, living in poverty.

The problems that face this child began long before he was born. Certainly there must be some type of justice. A crime has been committed. A television, a cell phone and some clothing have been stolen. Justice should be about the victims who lose things as a result of crimes. In this case, I see both families as victims, and attaining real justice for them does not seem to be a possibility in our society.

This case reminds me of another incident. Another member of the Society of African-American Police and I spend two hours handing out food and clothing at the North End Soup Kitchen on a cold winter day. We coordinate the effort along with many local businesses that donate the items. The North End Soup Kitchen is located in a predominately black section of town. The overwhelming majority of the people standing in the long lines are African-American women, many of whom I have seen on the streets in one fashion or another.

It is important that police in urban communities take the opportunity to show, especially to the poorest citizens, a different side of themselves. Many of the people standing in 20 degree weather are pleased to see the police interacting with them in a different, more humanitarian capacity. As I help one woman carry items to her car, she thanks me for not having her 12-year-old son locked away in a detention center for a breaking and entering charge. She states that he has gone to court and is now in a mentoring program that seems to be doing him some good. As she drives away, I think of how she and her six children still have a rough life ahead of them. The food and clothing she has just received will only make a tiny dent. I am proud to say that I am part of an effort that at least did that much.

TEN

The Poverty Trap

IT IS mid-December and my partner and I receive a call to make a welfare check in a predominately black, high-crime area. A school bus driver can't drop off a disabled child because the mother can't be located. The bus is sitting in front of the home, and lights are on inside. The driver has knocked at the door several times, but there is no answer. The driver finds this extremely suspicious because the mother has always been home when the child is dropped off. The driver fears the mother may have been injured inside.

The house appears to be abandoned, except for the lights on inside. It is a large, white house in dire need of a paint job. I see rotting wood in many places, and large piles of dry leaves surround it on all sides. An old abandoned car sits in front of a dilapidated garage.

All of the doors on the home are locked, and there doesn't appear to be forced entry. I consider the possibility of forcing entry to the house to be sure the mother is not inside and injured, but I don't really think I can justify damaging the property just because the mother may be irresponsible on this day. In this situation, there are no set rules or guidelines to help an officer make a decision that is 100 percent guaranteed. An officer can only rely on instinct and intuition. All things considered, my gut feeling is that the mother is not inside, but just why she isn't here is a pressing question. It is now 6 p.m. The driver has been here for three hours.

If the mother is not located, the question is what to do with the child. Since no family members are available to take her in, my decision is to call Children's Protective Services to ensure that the child at least has a safe place to live for the time being. The driver has been held long past her normal work hours. I need to relieve her of the responsibility. Just as I pick up my cell phone to call Children's Protective Services, the mother walks down the sidewalk with her arms filled with grocery bags.

She explains that her 15-year-old son is supposed to be home to sit with the handicapped child until she returns. She is on welfare and has no transportation. She had an appointment with a state agency designed to help her find employment. After completing her appointment with the agency, she had to get food for dinner, and to accomplish this she had to ride mass transportation.

Her 15-year-old son does not attend school and obviously does not follow her instructions. Because she says she doesn't trust anyone to properly care for her special-needs daughter, she refuses to work. To say that her daily life is difficult is an understatement. If I contact Children's Protective Services because I initially assume she is a negligent mother, I will only add to her daily burden. Having the police at her home because she fell short just this once must only add to her stress.

She exhales as she sets the groceries on the porch. Next, she labors to help her daughter off the bus and into the home. Before she gets the daughter situated, she drags the groceries off the porch into the house. Every facet of her life seems to be a chore. I want to do more to help, but I can't. This reality leaves me emotionally empty. The mother and child are safe together, but I wonder if they are happy. I wonder if they have ever had, or ever will have, a happy life.

ELEVEN

New Year, Old Problem

IT IS New Year's Eve. Near the end of our shift, my partner and I are dispatched to a domestic violence call from a young girl at a pay phone. She says her mother, who is seven months pregnant, is being beaten with a stick by her ex-boyfriend.

When we arrive, we find the woman bleeding from the right side of her head. She has several swellings the size of small eggs on her forearms. The wounds on her arms are defensive. She states that she used her arms to protect the child inside her. She is also bleeding from the right leg. Her ex-boyfriend has struck her more than 20 times with the stick. She ended a relationship with this man more than two months ago, but he still breaks into the home and assaults her.

On this day, he has kicked in the front door. I have taken a report from this woman before, for a beating by the same man. Last time, he broke out a window on the enclosed porch at the front of the home. As I take the new report, I notice that the window is still broken from the previous case. The glass from the broken window is still lying on the floor of the porch. The thin plastic blinds covering the broken window are still bent in the same positions. Whenever I patrol past this home, the sight of those crooked blinds disturbs me. It is but a small indication that perhaps the broken lives of most poor black people I meet are never repaired.

I think about how the unborn child inside the mother will be affected by the violence. How must a child inside a battered mother feel? What emotions must be transferred from that mother to the child during such an event? How will the life of a child who has literally experienced violence before birth be affected? What kind of life will that child eventually lead? I wonder what type of life society is creating for poor blacks in urban America.

The father who beat the mother of his child with the stick is a drug dealer. He has spent eight years in prison on drug charges. He is 31 years old. The mother is 33 years old, and unemployed with three children, counting the one she is expecting.

As I speak to her in the rear of an ambulance, she states, "I don't want to bring the New Year in like this." A new year is supposed to represent a new start, but for this woman it is just another day. How much hope can she have for what the year will bring when she is sitting in the back of an ambulance, injured, making a police report for domestic violence? The paramedics ask her to move her fingers and wrist to see if she has any broken bones. I meet her later at the hospital where doctors say the baby is not injured. She will need to spend at least another hour in observation before she can have her other wounds checked. Before she is done, she will undoubtedly "bring the New Year in like this."

TWELVE

But I Love Him

MY PARTNER and I are informed by dispatch that a man has pointed a shotgun at his wife. The woman has left the home and gone to a neighbor's house. When we arrive, we park a few houses down the street. The street is dark because streetlights are not working. As we approach the house on foot, we see the man place a shotgun in the trunk of a car. We arrest him and find his wife at the neighbor's home a few doors down the street.

Her face is bloodied with multiple cuts and bruises. She is lying on the neighbor's couch, trembling in fear. She says her husband has accused her of having an affair. He placed the barrel of the shotgun to her right temple and told her he wanted a divorce. He then struck her across her back with the barrel of the shotgun, knocking her to the floor. While on the floor, he beat her in the face with his fists. He grabbed a hammer from the dresser and struck her once on the right arm. Then he went to the kitchen and returned with a knife and began swinging it at her. When she raised her hands to defend herself, she was cut on the left hand. Eventually, she was able to run to the neighbor's house.

An ambulance takes the woman to the hospital. My partner and I collect the shotgun, hammer and knife as evidence. The scene is photographed and processed by someone from the Identification Bureau. The evidence is passed to a detective, who then takes it to the prosecutor.

Months later, when the case goes to court, the stage is set for successful prosecution of the husband. However, the woman denies the story, the case is dismissed, and the woman and her husband leave the courtroom holding hands. I am left sitting in a room with the detective and the prosecutor. We are stunned. All have done their jobs to protect the victim, but it doesn't solve the problem. She no longer wants or feels that she needs protection from the system, and though it seems sad, it is her right. This is a classic case of how many victims of domestic violence refuse to prosecute their attackers.

Later, my partner and I go to a similar call.

The night is quiet and so far uneventful. Five inches of snow have fallen on what has been an otherwise mild Michigan winter day. The city for a moment comes to a peaceful standstill. The streetlights illuminate the large snowflakes that still fall. It's near the end of the shift and the roads are filled with snow. I begin to drive slowly back to the station when my partner and I are dispatched to check for a black woman lying in the snow.

When we arrive, we find a black man holding her limp body in the middle of the street. They are both known drug addicts. Finally the man lays her down in the middle of the cold street. Her right eye is swollen shut. She is frail and weak and can barely talk, but she says enough to let us know that the man we saw holding her has assaulted her. He is her boyfriend. I have arrested him on another occasion for assaulting the woman. We arrest him again and talk to several neighbors who saw but didn't see. They don't want to be involved.

My partner turns on the emergency lights so that the woman will not be hit by traffic. An ambulance is en route but we don't want to move her, not knowing what other injuries she may have. I kneel beside her as she lies here in the fetal position on the cold snowy street in 17-degree weather. She is a woman barely over 40 who appears to be every bit of 70. Her hair is short and uncombed. Her cheekbones protrude over her sunken jaws because she has no teeth.

Finally the ambulance arrives and takes her away. My partner and I take the man to jail for domestic violence, where he will spend the usual 20 hours. I think the chances of this woman following through with the complaint are slim to none. She is always either drunk or high. My thought is that she would never be able to articulate her problem to a detective, prosecutor or judge.

Much to my surprise, my partner and I received subpoenas for court on her case. However, predictably, we see the case dismissed as the woman denies the story and walks out of the courtroom holding hands with her assailant.

In another domestic assault case, we find a single, black, unemployed mother of four who has been beaten in the presence of her children by her black live-in boyfriend, who is the biological father of only her youngest child.

They began arguing because the man had stayed away for most of the day and returned home intoxicated. When the woman questioned him about his activity, he struck her several times in the face with his fist as the children watched. He is an unemployed drug user. He leaves before we arrive, so no arrest is made.

As we leave this call, I see the woman's oldest child, a 10-year-old boy, outside dribbling a basketball in a carefree manner. He has mastered handling that basketball, through the legs, behind the back, with both hands. Sometimes he is low to ground. Other times he stands upright, but he never loses control. I think that perhaps he has also mastered coping with seeing his mother abused, but how long can he control the feelings he must have about it? What kind of man will he become as a result of this exposure? Only time will tell.

I realize it is my personal need to resolve these cases, and my inability to do so that causes my hurt. Domestic cases in particular are perhaps the greatest example that no amount of effort by an individual or the system can save people from self-destruction.

THIRTEEN

Grief of a Childless Father

WE DRIVE to an unusual call at a cemetery. A man has found what he thinks are the skeletal remains of an infant. I speak to the young black male, age 24, who has twin infants buried here. He states that the boy and girl twins died a day after they were born four months premature on this same day three years ago. He says he visits the grave site every year on this date. As he points to the tiny red flag marking the grave of his children, he explains that he and his girlfriend can't afford headstones for the children. On this day while visiting the grave he notices a skeleton just a few feet from the grave of his children.

I view the remains and cannot determine if they are human. I see partial leg and thighbones, a pelvis, a spine and a rib cage. No head or arms can be found. No fur is found that would confirm it is an animal. Just before receiving the call, a snowstorm began. Six to 12 inches are expected. Had the man not reported the bones, the remains would be covered in snow very soon. Homicide detectives come to the location, and they can't positively rule that the remains are human.

After a crime scene technician photographs the remains, my partner and I drive the bones to a local hospital where a doctor views them and officially pronounces them dead. He states that he doesn't think they are human, but he will leave it in the morgue for a pathologist to make an official determination.

By the time I complete the report for this call, my shift is finished. I think how sad it would be if someone had actually killed an infant in a cemetery. Also, I think about the irony of a grieving father finding a skeleton near the grave of his children. Most of all, I am bothered by the thought of a grieving father who actually loves his children and can't afford headstones for them.

After some time, it is determined that the bones are those of an animal. Perhaps it was just the loving heart of a grieving father that made them appear to be bones of a child.

FOURTEEN

Six Months Later

IT IS a Sunday. I am at the station for an arrest, and I can sneak a peak at a televised football game in another room. After completing a report for a domestic violence arrest, I am ordered to assist in processing the arrest of a 22-year-old black woman who is soon to be interrogated about the shooting of her boyfriend.

I go to a private room in the detective bureau where interrogations can be seen on a television monitor. I see a young black woman sitting and talking with detectives. I recognize her as the same young pregnant black woman I saw standing in the crowd at the homicide scene of the two young men six months before. I leave the room a few times to get an update on the game before I finally become more interested in this new game that is her interrogation. I am sure the outcome will be more important and dramatic than the best football game.

I think back to the day of the homicides. I think about the irony of how this young woman was pregnant at that time and is now being held for possibly murdering someone's son. I remember how she stood out in that crowd because she was young, beautiful and pregnant.

On this day I see her in another light. She is crying and pleading in an interview room as her boyfriend is lying in the hospital on life support. According to reports, he has already died twice in the trauma room. Twice, medical personnel have had the stainless steel cart waiting to take him to the morgue and twice he fought off death.

Earlier today paramedics found him face down in his own blood with a handgun in each of his coat pockets. As it turns out, one of them was used to shoot him in the chest.

It is said that confession is good for the soul. I watch as the woman waives her right to an attorney. Maybe she needs to confess. Talking may seem the proper thing to do. For her it may provide a sense of relief, or maybe she just feels compelled to help the police. I am unsure. Regardless of her rationale, she is a suspect, and giving statements without legal representation can prove detrimental.

I am sure she doesn't know the magnitude of what it means to give a statement without legal representation. I suspect many young black people have and will find themselves in this situation. It does not suggest that anyone should lie to the police. In fact, making false reports to police is a crime. However, silence is a right that can't be legally perceived as guilt. A person is innocent until proven guilty. The burden of proof is on police and prosecutors. I wonder how many young African-Americans really know their rights even after they have been read a Miranda warning?

The detectives have their suspicions about her, but without her confession they really would have a difficult time establishing a case against her. However, she confesses. The detectives have done their jobs. At a later time she will find it hard to refute what she has told them.

After the interview she talks to me as I process her. She is working a decent job at a local factory. She has two small children she thinks she will never see again. I tell her to think positively, though I know she has every reason to be afraid. Her boyfriend is still living. What she has done isn't murder yet.

I tell her I remember seeing her at that homicide scene back in the summer and she says that she also remembers seeing me there. She tells me that the child she was pregnant with then is just two months old now. The boyfriend she shot is the father of this child. He had given her a sexually transmitted disease, which could have caused the baby to be born blind. As she talks, I can't help but think how this infant could very well lose both parents today. If the father dies and the mother goes to prison for killing him, where will this leave either of her children? It will be one hell of a legacy to leave for them.

The young woman tells me how her boyfriend has physically abused her. She is the breadwinner for the family. The boyfriend works occasionally at a corner store, but has never had what she calls a real job. He has cheated on her constantly and on this day she catches him cheating again. She confronts him. They both have guns. She says he threatens to kill her. He places his hand in his right coat pocket as if to reach for a gun. Beating him to the punch, she draws her gun and shoots him once in the chest. He falls to the floor. In a panic, not knowing what else to do, she places her gun on him and flees to ask a neighbor to call 9-1-1.

Later, she shows up at the hospital to inquire about her boyfriend's condition and is arrested on suspicion of attempted murder. I think again about her confession. Is it really a confession or does an element of self-defense exist? Would other extenuating or mitigating circumstances have helped her had she remained silent, or am I just being overly sympathetic to her cause?

When I finish processing her, my partner and I drive her to the county jail. I don't want to see her get away with the crime, and I don't want her to go to prison. I'm sure she is a victim of physical and emotional abuse. She has said that all she wants is to keep her family together. Even though she is not married, she considers what she has a family. She comes from a broken home. She doesn't know her father. She needs a sense of family. However, at the moment she is the least of the victims in the scenario. Her boyfriend is in emergency surgery, and her children will spend maybe the first of many nights without her.

I walk her inside the county jail. She is dressed in the orange jump suit the detectives provided. I tell her to sit on a bench, and I notice her innocent look. It is far from the face of a black criminal that usually is depicted to the public. I say goodbye to her as a deputy seizes her. The following day her boyfriend dies. Usually, I find myself wishing for something, but in this case, I don't know what to wish for.

FIFTEEN

Who‗s going to help me?

ON OUR last call of the night, my partner and I are
called to assist the black mother of a violent 14-year-
old girl. Dispatch says the girl has ransacked the house
and locked herself in a bathroom. When we arrive, we
find a mother who is a recovering drug addict, and
who seems to be doing the very best she can to set a
good example for her six children. The mother is very
articulate. She works part time and attends school. She
is raising the children alone, and that isn't easy.

In my line of work, I find that asking the
whereabouts of the father is a redundant question that
has four typical answers: in jail, on drugs in jail, on
drugs somewhere on the streets, or dead. After a while
both the question and the answers are painful to me,
so I can imagine how the mothers and children must
feel. Most times when I ask a black woman the
question, the facial expressions she makes before she
speaks say "come on now, you know the story, but if I
must spell it out, I will." However futile, it is still an
important part of the story.

Also, when I spend only a few moments with a family in crisis, it is hard for me to glean every little thing I need to know to make a valid assessment of what is really going on. How long has the mother been clean? What lasting negative impression has she made on her children before she cleaned up? Once parents show weaknesses, children are often hurt, unforgiving, and rebellious. Then society preaches to children that they should respect their parents no matter what pain the parents have inflicted upon them. We, in effect, ask children not to judge their parents' behavior simply because they are adults. At the same time, we place the behavior of children under a microscope. However, in today's world, this is a tough sell. Needless to say, children find this hypocritical.

In this case, the cycle repeats itself. The mother shares that the daughter has been experimenting with marijuana. She was a good basketball player and an honor roll student one year ago. Now she has quit the team and is also repeating the eighth grade.

My partner, who is a black single mother, takes charge of the call. She takes the tough love approach and makes the woman's daughter clean up the house, get her school clothes ready for the following day, and go to bed. It is past 11 p.m. My partner becomes the de facto parent for the hour we spend on this call. However, as deeply as we may feel for this woman, we can't raise her children for her.

The mother has her work cut out for her. Her problems don't stop with the 14-year-old. Her 16-year-old pregnant daughter is lying on the living room couch. Her 12-year-old son refuses to go to bed, and two other smaller children are crying about one thing or another.

She sums up her experience this way: "I've done everything I can. They don't listen to me. If I could put them all on the street right now, I would, but you would get me for abandonment or neglect. I've been abandoned, I've been neglected, and who's going to help me?"

SIXTEEN

A Lesson in Dying

I RECEIVE a call to proceed to the emergency room for a death investigation. Dead bodies make me cringe more than any other thing. Will there be trauma, bloating, decomposition? How bad will it smell? Will I have to touch it? Will emotional family members be present? These things all play inside my mind every time I get one of these calls. I am unsure how I will cope with any combination of these things. All I can do is show up and deal with whatever the situation presents in the best way I can. It is yet something else that can't be taught or learned in a police academy or a lecture hall.

On this day, I must examine the body of a middle-aged black woman. She has been transported to the hospital in full cardiac arrest. A nurse directs me to a small brightly lit room with pastel painted walls. The woman's body lies on the stainless steel cart. She is covered to her chest in a white sheet. She appears peaceful, yet she appears to have had a hard life. She has aged well beyond her 49 years. Though I see no visible trauma, life has left its mark on her. She has a history of heart problems, kidney failure, high blood pressure, diabetes and seizures. She has no family doctor. Her residence is listed as the Berridge Hotel, a local "flop house" for the down and out. My father once lived there, and I visited him years ago. As a police officer, I have frequently been called to the Berridge, for everything from assaults, to robberies and drug trafficking. The Berridge is not a nice place to have listed as an address at the time of death. Her family has already come and gone. There is no dramatic emotional production.

Later, I read the woman's obituary. It says that she had been a lifelong resident of Flint, and had been employed for four years at McDonald's. She enjoyed bingo, music and watching television. She was a caring mother and good at heart. She enjoyed her family and would be missed. She left behind a husband who lives in Indiana, four adult children and 18 grandchildren.

Despite the recent circumstances of her living and dying, above all, she was a human being.

SEVENTEEN

Child Unprotected

MY DAY has been relatively quiet and slow until I am dispatched to a local hospital to assist with an 8-year-old black boy who has been raped by a 36-year-old black man who is a "friend" of the family.

The little boy has already told his story to one white male detective who is trying to force him to repeat it to another white male detective. The boy, who was once wide-eyed and smiling, has become somber and places his head on the table where he is sitting and tunes out the world. He refuses to speak anymore.

When both detectives leave the room, the child and I strike up a conversation. I tell him I have three children close to his age, and this seems to interest him. His eyes brighten again and his smile returns. He sits up straight once more.

"How old are your kids?" he asks excitedly.

"I have twin 9-year-olds in fourth grade and one 11-year-old in sixth grade," I tell him.

"Do they got a game? I got a Dreamcast," he says.

"My kids have... " I paused to recall.

"A PlayStation!" he correctly interjects. "Everybody got a PlayStation," he continues. "What are their favorite games to play?"

"I bought the Matrix. They like that," I tell him.

"The Matrix Reloaded," he clarifies for me.

He tells me he was playing video games when the man made him get down on his knees and perform oral sex on him until he ejaculated in his mouth. He tells me the man also used his finger to penetrate his buttocks during the oral sex.

"He told me that he would cut my head off if I didn't do it," the boy says. "He called me the B word and punched me in both sides of my face with his fist."

The boy also tells me that the man had sexually assaulted him on four other occasions. The hospital is able to pull up his records to confirm his statement. Why someone hadn't protected this child before now is beyond me.

I sit with the doctor as he examines the boy's body for signs of trauma. His mouth is swabbed for evidence of semen. I collect swabs and his clothing as evidence. As I wait with him while Children's Protective Services talks with his mother and detectives, he is very active and animated. He displays his Spiderman routine in which he pretends to shoot a web from his wrist at a male nurse who is down the hall. When the nurse obliges him and pretends to shoot back, the limber boy, in order to duck the on-coming imaginary web, leans backward while keeping his feet on the floor and touches the palms of his hands on the floor behind him, never once losing his balance.

"He missed me," he states, with a wide, victorious grin.

A nurse brings us both juice and Graham crackers. He gets a kick out of me eating and drinking with him. I hurt for the boy who has somehow learned not to show hurt at all. He never cries or has any outward expression of grief, pain or anger about his situation. However, at some point, when he is an adult, he will deal with those emotions. What type of adult will this make him? What price will society pay for producing a poor black male child who is repeatedly raped by a black adult while being raised in a housing project by a mother who is an unemployed drug user? I think of my own children and hope they will never in their lifetime encounter a sexual predator. After this experience, I fear for the safety of all children in this world.

After talking to detectives and the boy's mother, Children's Protective Services decides to remove the child from the home. Separating children from their parents is always an emotionally wrenching event, even when the child has been abused. The mother and child hug and cry before he is taken away. I never say goodbye to him. I am not sure if I avoid saying goodbye so that I won't see him hurt anymore, or so I won't feel more hurt.

I meet the detectives who tell me they suspect the mother is prostituting the boy.

EIGHTEEN

The Breaking Point

WE RESPOND to a call for a welfare check of an elderly black male. For me, policing is a process of developing emotional tolerance for abnormal experiences. However, no matter how well one learns to cope with the abnormal, usually one type of call still haunts an officer more than it haunts others. My greatest demon is the welfare check and the possibility of finding a dead person. I'm not sure I can beat it. The mere mention of it by a dispatcher strikes fear in my heart. No matter how slowly I drive, I always arrive too quickly on the scene.

We arrive on this call and find three distraught women. Two are daughters and one is a sister of the man who hasn't been heard from in more than a week. His car sits in his driveway. One woman tries his number on her cell phone, but he still doesn't answer. I have no suggestions. The only thing left to do is force entry to the man's home to see if he's inside. The possibility always exists that he could be out riding with someone, but the family knows his habits. They know he never rides with anyone.

I am the senior officer on the scene, which means I not only have a responsibility to the family, but I also must show my partner the proper way to handle this call, his first of this type. The family has no keys to the house and bars cover the windows and doors. I use a crowbar to pry open the bars to the front door. I kick the inner door as close to the doorknob as possible. Doors open easier this way. Once the door is open, I yell, "Flint Police!" in the event the man is alive with a weapon and not in his right mind. I also want to hear any sudden movement by a possible criminal. As I wait for a response to my shouting, all I hear is a dead silence. All I see before me is darkness, though the sun still shines outside. My feeling is a bad one.

Instinctively, I begin to look for a body. I wait for the smell of death, but it doesn't come. As my partner and I use flashlights to search, everything seems to be in place. Nothing is ransacked. No furniture is overturned. As we pass through the living room, I see mail on the dining room table. My partner follows my every footstep. Family members are anxiously yelling outside at the door, asking if we have found anything. I yell to them to stay out of the house until we complete the search. As I move toward the kitchen, I brace myself for what I might find, but I find nothing.

Family members are becoming more anxious. I yell again to them to stay out. At the same time, I am still listening for any suspicious sounds.

I walk through the dining room to a long hallway with two bedrooms on either end and a bathroom between. Each of the three doors is closed. I kick open one bedroom door and find nothing. I instruct my partner to watch the bathroom door. I then kick open the other bedroom door and find nothing again. Finally, I throw my shoulder into the bathroom door and it barely moves. I can feel the weight of something against it. I throw my shoulder against the door again and it opens an inch. I strike the door again and open it enough to get my head inside. I look toward the floor and see the man's body collapsed against the door. His pants are down around his ankles. I can see that he has bled from the nose. He is bloated and his body fluids have run across the floor. The bathroom is small. I push the door open enough to be sure no one else is inside with him.

I walk back toward the front door where the man's family waits. By now they are on edge and desperate.

"Did you find him?"

"Is he OK?"

"Is he in there?"

They all shout as one woman gently touches my hand with hers. No doctor, paramedic, social worker, counselor or funeral director is on the scene to give the bad news. It is my job. I then speak the five most painful and difficult words I have ever spoken during my career.

"I'm sorry ma'am; he's deceased."

How I find the courage to speak those words, I don't know. I only know that those words come from the deepest place of hurt that exists inside a human being. Those words are a breaking point for that family and for me. They are followed by screams.

"Where is he in the house?"

"Did someone hurt him?"

"What do you mean, he's deceased?"

"Are you sure?"

"Oh my God, no!"

One woman wants to see her father, but I convince her that it is best that she doesn't see him like this. As I walk the woman back out to the yard, I see that more than 40 family members have gathered. Questions come from all directions. People mourn as though a funeral is taking place at this moment.

Paramedics arrive to remove the body. An ambulance parks in the driveway. My partner and I keep the family from entering the home while paramedics work. One thing I can't bear to watch is a human being placed in a body bag, so I stay away. When they move the body, the odor comes, as if meat in a large freezer has spoiled. As the paramedics place the body in the ambulance, many of the family members place their hands on the vehicle, as if they are touching the dead man. Even as the ambulance drives slowly down the street, some family members walk behind it with their hands still touching.

The ambulance begins to drive faster and the people remove their hands and stand in the middle of the street and watch until it disappears. I try to process the emotion from this call and I feel faint. My legs weaken as I walk to my cruiser to have a seat. I'm afraid, because the last thing I need to do is fall to the ground before the very people who depend on me for strength in their time of crisis. I reach my cruiser and my heart is racing and I am lightheaded. I want to cry, but I can't. It is difficult for me not to mourn a little bit when I watch so many people mourn so dramatically. It is impossible to fight off the thoughts of what it would be like to lose one of my own loved ones in this manner.

The nature of my being in authority means I must suppress my own natural human emotion. At this moment, I realize that if I had to handle this type of call every day, I would have to quit my job. For the first time, I question whether I am in the right profession. I think about quitting right here and now, but I suck it up and prepare to take the next call. I realize this can be a breaking point for me, but I am not ready to be broken. At least not today, anyway.

NINETEEN

The Little Things

AT THE very start of my shift, a young black male wearing a Navy R.O.T.C. uniform flags my partner and me down near a downtown fast-food restaurant. He has missed his ride home from school and still has a long way to go.

Sometimes a fine line exists between providing a meaningful service and being a taxicab. It is getting dark. Giving him a ride ensures that he will be safe. It is a proactive, preventative decision, as opposed to a reactive situation where the child is missing, the mother is frantic, and the already diminished police resources are further stressed in an investigation.

We drive the child home, where the mother has already become worried. She is grateful that we have taken the time to bring him home. Many people assume that the police would have more important or more serious things to do, but what is more important than keeping a child safe? Furthermore, the child is pleasant and focused on his future. He has dreams of being a military man, and he is actively working toward that goal. In his own bashful, unassuming way, he smashes the stereotype. Unfortunately, it is a rare but refreshing encounter with a young black male in urban America who hasn't succumbed to the lure of crime, gangs, guns, and drugs. He lives in a high-crime area and he has no father figure.

Just as we finish with this family, we receive another call involving a missing 13-year-old black boy. We are told to meet a cab driver at a gas station near a busy intersection. We find him, and the boy is sitting in the rear of his taxi. He tells us he saw the child wandering and became concerned and picked him up. The boy is lost. He is looking for his church, but he can't remember the name or the location of the church. He is a nice kid, though he seems mentally slow. His personal hygiene is very poor, and his clothes are old and tattered.

We check his name through L.E.I.N. (Law Enforcement Information Network), to determine if he is listed as a missing person or a runaway, but he is not. I ask him for his home phone and address. I talk to his brother who confirms that he should be at church. His mother is not home. He gives me a cell phone number, where I finally contact the mother at another address. She says he should have been home waiting for the church van to pick him up. Apparently the child just got impatient and took off walking because the van didn't arrive in what he thought was a timely manner.

We drive the child to his mother, who is very upset with him. She is poor and raising eight children alone, which explains the child's outward appearance. She says he is having trouble in school. However, the important thing is that the child is safe. Just as a concerned cab driver picked up this child, a pedophile could easily have done the same.

Once again, in the world of law enforcement, this would not qualify as a major investigation. There was no high-speed chase, no shoot-out with the bad guy, no dead people, and no big arrest. However, a concerned citizen and the police working together in a small, extremely low-profile manner prevented the possibility of a tragedy. This investigation holds no less importance than those that frequently make the news or television shows. Furthermore, this is more likely the type of police work an officer may do on a daily basis, as opposed to the other more glamorized activity for which police have unfortunately become known in American society.

TWENTY

Children of Destiny

NIGHTFALL IS nearly here. I am working alone when a unit calls for assistance on a traffic stop. Five or more people occupy an old gray van. The thought of an ambush looms in my mind. The traffic stop is said to be the most dangerous activity police officers undertake. Vans increase that danger greatly. Compared to cars, vans can have more doors and more room to hide people and weapons.

A citizen suspects that drugs are being sold from this van and has called 9-1-1. When I arrive, I assist the other officers in removing the people from the vehicle. We find five black males inside. The two youngest are 13 and 14, and the other three are in their 20s.

It is a growing trend that adult men now frequently hang out with underage boys. In today's black culture, sometimes little distinguishes a young teen male from a male in his 20s.

When I was growing up in the 1970s, a year or two age difference was considered huge. Without a doubt, teens and men in their 20s were not peers. In this new culture, black men in their 20s who are not dead or in prison are most times living in their mothers' homes. Many are ex-cons and/or unemployed. Socially they don't have much more status or power than teens. The teens who lack positive male influence find role models in men who can only teach them how to commit crime. The men who are many times on probation don't want to do more prison time, so they coerce teens into committing crimes. Though many teens are also on probation, the system is less likely to place them in prison than it would the adult male. Many teens in this culture, like their older companions, have already created a track record that will likely prevent them from attending colleges and working at meaningful jobs.

I assist in transporting the teens to the station where they are eventually booked for carrying a concealed weapon, possession with intent to deliver drugs, felony firearm, and maintaining a drug vehicle. The 13-year-old boy is only five feet tall and weighs a mere 90 pounds. This is his first arrest. However, the 14-year-old already has a criminal history. He is on probation for not attending school. During the booking procedure, I find that he can't spell his street name, the name of his city, or his school name. Education is yet another casualty of the culture. This, combined with criminal activity, helps seal the fate of many young black men. Thus, many are destined to live a life of crime, spend many years in prison, or die an early death.

Period.

TWENTY-ONE

Nowhere to Play

WE CHECK on some suspicious people at a street corner and find four innocent little black boys playing in an abandoned house. We explain to them the dangers of playing in the house and tell them that some officers might even arrest them for breaking and entering.

As the boys find their way home, my partner and I count 14 abandoned homes on the street. At the end of the block is a dilapidated apartment complex in which many of the apartments are abandoned. The children have no safe place to play in this neighborhood. While many will debate how the conditions of this neighborhood came to be, it is obvious to me that it is something unique to black urban life.

In an unrelated case, I am working alone when I am dispatched to a breaking and entering in progress. I am just clearing a call on the southwest side of town. The breaking and entering is located near the extreme northern border of the city, and the police department is short-staffed. Another officer, who is also working alone on northwest side of town, is dispatched to the same call.

Further information from dispatch reveals that a woman entered her home and found young black males inside. They ran from the house upon seeing her. She chased them and caught one. Neighbors caught another boy, but released him before police arrived because our response time was slow.

When we arrive, we find the woman holding a 13-year-old boy. The boy is already on probation for armed robbery and is in possession of marijuana. He gives us the names and addresses of other boys involved. They live on the street that contains the 14 abandoned houses. The other officer and I conduct a follow-up investigation and we find many of the stolen items described by the woman. Two of the suspects, a 15-year-old and a 12-year-old, sit in the middle of their living room floor playing a video game they stole from the home. They have it connected to a small television. They are brothers in a family of eight children. They are surrounded on all sides by siblings waiting their turn to play.

When we speak to the mother, she pretends not to know how the game and other items got into the house, though she obviously knows she didn't buy them. When parents lose control of their children, they start to turn a blind eye and a deaf ear, and in a sense become helpless.

The other officer and I arrest the two boys and seize the stolen items. We take the mother with us because she has no transportation. A detective will need her permission to interview her children and the process will be prolonged if we wait for her to find her own ride to the station. We inform the mother that we can charge her with possession of the stolen goods as well, but we won't do it because she is cooperative with the investigation.

Once at the station, I find that the boys can't read. They don't know their middle names and are unsure of their own birth dates. They don't know their address or phone number. Their personal hygiene is very poor. Their clothes are filthy, and they can't recall the last time they had a bath. The 15-year-old is still in the eighth grade. Among the things they stole from the house is a package of lunch meat.

All of the boys are charged with felony home invasion. The family court orders that the 13-year-old be lodged in a juvenile detention center. The brothers are released to their mother.

As the other officer and I drive the 13-year-old to the detention center, we stop at a street corner barbecue stand to grab a bite to eat. I ask the boy if he is hungry and he tells me he hasn't eaten all day. I share a polish sausage sandwich with him and give him a soft drink. I take the long way to the detention center to give him a chance to finish it all.

I try to imagine how this child can have a positive future. I believe the only way I can positively impact him is to treat him nicely when he least deserves it. I feel that if I treat him like a child instead of a criminal, he might remember. If he should ever overcome the armed robbery, the home invasion, and the possession of marijuana charges, he might remember that somebody really cares. Finally, I think that if he ever finds himself in a position of authority, perhaps he will do the same. Based upon what I know of the outcome of many children in his situation, I know my actions are a long shot. Yet, when I think of all the wayward children in the world, I have to believe a small few actually change their lives. It must be that their success stories are just never told. I find myself hoping that maybe this kid is one of those few.

TWENTY-TWO

The Lost Daughter

WHILE WORKING alone, I am dispatched to a liquor store to meet a black father who needs assistance to pick up his runaway daughter at an address not far from the store. Many drug-related shootings and stabbings have occurred in the parking lot of the store. Next door sits a funeral home. Directly across the street sits a black Baptist church. On M. L. King Avenue, these three institutions encompass the extent of the poor black culture: drugs, alcohol, violence, death, funerals and religion, and this is where a father wants to meet police to find his lost daughter.

When the father doesn't show, I go to the address he has given me and I find him. He states that his 13-year-old daughter continually runs away from home and refuses to go to school. She also smokes cigarettes and marijuana. In addition, she has a 6-month-old baby. When I locate her, she states that the father drinks heavily and threatens violence against her when he is drunk. She runs away because she fears the father when he is in this condition.

Though a crime has not been committed on this day, a breakdown exists between the father and his daughter. She does not want to go home with him. I drive the child to the police station and contact Children's Protective Services to determine if they will place this child in emergency foster care. They refuse. I have no choice but to drive the child home. Once there, I speak with the father again. He and his live-in girlfriend have four children in the home. Times are hard for them. His girlfriend is unemployed and he works only three hours a day in the lunchroom at a younger child's elementary school where he earns minimum wage. I am familiar with the school because I recently volunteered there. More than 400 children in that school share the same socioeconomic background.

The father gives me a brief history of his volatile family situation. He admits that he has abandoned his girlfriend and children many times. When he returned the last time, he found that his youngest daughter was pregnant. He expresses a desire to repair the damage done to his family, but it seems an impossible task. Finally, as we end our conversation, he voices his regrets. "When I left my family, I thought when I came back they would always be the same, but now I see that things will never be the same again. They will never be the same."

TWENTY-THREE

The Discarded Child

MY PARTNER and I are dispatched to assist Children's Protective Services in removing a 1-year-old child from a home. When we arrive, we find a large, dilapidated home with a trash-filled yard. The house looks abandoned. No one answers the door for the social workers but they still suspect someone is inside. In a last-ditch effort to rouse whoever might be inside, I pound on the door with my fist. The noise creates the impression that the door may be forced open. Most people are startled or agitated by this type of knock and feel compelled to respond out of anger or fear. In this case, a sheepish looking black man comes to the door. His thick hair is uncombed and matted to his head. His beard is long and scraggily, and his clothes are dirty and torn. The social worker informs him that they have been ordered by the court to take the child. The man does not speak, but he is cooperative.

We enter the home and it is easy to see why the child is being taken. Foul odors of trash, urine, alcohol and rotting food permeate everything. The carpets are stained and beer bottles of various sizes are scattered on the floor and the furniture. There is no electricity, heat or water. In the kitchen, the oven door on the gas stove is open and the burners on the stove are lit. This is the only source of heat.

The parents of the child are unemployed drug addicts. Their home has become a place where other neighborhood addicts come to get high. One such black female addict sits on the couch and stares into space as we search the home for the baby. The mother of the child hasn't been seen in months. We find the child lying on a bed in a room filled with dirty clothing. She has no baby bed. When asked where the baby sleeps, the father replies, "She sleeps in the bed with me." Statistics indicate that in Genesee county, African-American babies die three times more often than others, and partly for this reason by suffocation.

When the young social workers ask for the baby's bottle, the father gives them an encrusted bottle containing spoiled milk. Without looking at the bottle, one of the social workers tries to feed the baby with it. Before I can stop her, the baby jerks her head away. I can tell that neither of the social workers have children.

We secure the child and exit the house. I watch as the social workers struggle to place the baby in a car seat. As a parent of three children, I recognize their awkwardness. Once the social workers get the baby in the car seat, they can't get the tiny metal buckle to lock between the baby's legs. I can see the frustration on their faces. I walk over and snap it in place for them. This is the very nature of human service professions. A particular type of awkwardness always exists in handling human life, and though certain life experiences prepare us better than others, we can never become totally comfortable with everything we will be asked to do. Nor can we be trained for every possible scenario we will face. Still, we find a way to do whatever it is we are charged to do on a particular day. Our only preparation is experience.

We talk for a moment about how shameful it is that any child lives in these conditions. By now, the child is smiling as only a 1-year-old child can under these circumstances. This says to me that children are born happy. The world makes them sad.

Just after I notice the child smiling, I see the father and the unknown woman walk away from the home, probably in search of their next high. The social workers drive past me with the child.

I fight back tears and prepare to take the next call, whatever it might be. This is the nature of the business.

TWENTY-FOUR

Same-Sex Debate

DISPATCH ASKS us to respond to a call for a 15-year-old black girl who is threatening to run away from home. I find a 33-year-old mother who begins our interaction by telling me that her daughter was once an honor roll student and a star basketball player, but she is now failing school and has been kicked off the basketball team. Eventually she shares that the biggest issue is that her daughter is gay. The mother is having a difficult time accepting it. Being gay is against the mother's moral beliefs. The mother says she was raised as a Christian and she has raised her daughter as a Christian. She says that a person can't be Christian and be gay. Accepting that her daughter is gay would mean that she would have to rethink her beliefs. Mother and daughter can't seem to reach any middle ground.

The mother blames society for influencing children. She talks about the increased exposure of gay and lesbian television shows and the social debate about same sex marriages. Locally, one gay male teen couple were featured in a Sunday newspaper. I made certain my children did not see that newspaper. Popular culture and the mass media have a way of bombarding the public with certain images. As a parent, I feel sex images may impact negatively on my children. I am not ready to explain to my children why boys date boys and why Madonna and Brittany Spears kissed on national television, or why Justin Timberlake exposed Janet Jackson's breast during the 2004 Super Bowl half-time show. As a parent, I find our nation's fixation with sexuality maddening. However, as a police officer, I must remain open-minded. I interact with gay and lesbian members of my community just as I do with other populations, and I find that their problems are no different from anyone else's. Also, I partnered for a year with a lesbian officer who I feel is one of the best partners I have ever had.

It is true that for teenagers today, being gay does not hold the same social stigma that it did in past decades. More and more teenagers, especially girls, are more open about this type of sexuality, leaving parents at a loss about how to react to it.

The mother in this case has had her daughter in counseling. A grandfather had once molested the daughter. The mother wants to believe that the daughter's behavior may be a result of the molestation.

The daughter says that her stress comes from trying to be something that she is not in order to please her mother, but in the process she only ends up being unhappy with herself for even trying. She says she has tried wearing "girlie" clothes and acting in a "girlie" way, but it just doesn't work. Additionally, she says that she is deeply in love with her girlfriend. It raises the question of whether or not people are born gay, or if it is a choice or dysfunction.

Many people who call the police into their home want guidance. After we listen, we often can advise them on a direct line of action. However, in this case I avoid giving advice because the conflict is so centered on personal beliefs, none of which fall into the neat boxes of right and wrong. The daughter says she was born gay and that God made her that way. The mother says that being gay is against God. The best I can do is suggest that they pray for some sort of resolution.

Before I received this call, I heard about a gang of gay high school girls who try to intimidate heterosexual girls into having homosexual encounters. This female aggression is a recent phenomenon and causes much debate among school administrators.

After this call, I realize that the problem this family faces is one that concerns many in the community. Even my fellow police officers are puzzled. I wonder where this is headed.

In an unrelated event, my partner and I are called for trouble with a man. Upon arrival, we find a short, small-framed black man looking sad and dejected and sitting on the steps of a home. Before we can speak to him, a much larger, more muscular black man walks out of the home and stands next to him. The body language of both men seems awkward. I can immediately sense an intimate connection between them. If I am to have any opportunity to solve a problem between them, I must know the true nature of the relationship. Before I can stop myself, I blurt, "Are you guys a couple?" Both men confirm my observation.

This is new territory for me. I have never dealt with two men who share an intimate relationship. I feel that it is the nature of being in authority that makes it necessary for me to shield my discomfort. Otherwise, I am not the experienced, expert, all-wise, all-knowing authoritarian citizens think they have called to resolve their problems.

The larger man states that he wants the other man to leave. He says he has a new lover and is breaking off the five-year relationship with the man who sits in desperation at his doorstep. The sitting man is more emotional and unwilling to leave. He cries openly and professes love for the man that seems as genuine as any I've seen expressed in heterosexual relationships.

His emotions strike me as strange and unnatural, yet I find myself respecting them and having the same compassion I would for a person in a heterosexual relationship. The miserable man states that he has been married to a woman for 16 years and has three children. I am curious as to how he wound up in this relationship, but I resist the urge to ask, as it is not relevant.

The man's biggest source of hurt is that his gay lover is his first and only. Additionally, he has invested time and thousands of dollars to support his lover who has trouble holding a job and makes a fool of him before their friends. I think that these dynamics are no different than man-woman relationships.

In the midst of this fight, regardless of the outcome, it has become clear to me that the concept of love, in all its joy and pain, between any two consenting people, can't be legislated, no matter what any of us believe.

TWENTY-FIVE

Another Trip to the Mental Ward

SOME DAYS seem to have a theme. Today, mental illness seems to be it. My partner and I receive a call about a mother having trouble with a 13-year-old boy.

When we arrive, we find that the boy, without being provoked, has become violent and verbally abusive to his mother and other family members. After wrestling a knife away from him, the mother called the police. We find him in the front yard cursing at the top of his voice while being restrained by his older brother. We handcuff him and transport him to the hospital for a mental evaluation.

Later we respond to a stabbing. I speak with the mother of a 17-year-old black male who became angry with his 10-year-old brother over a video game.

The 17-year-old grabbed a knife and poked the 10-year-old in the arm just enough to break the skin and cause bleeding. When the mother tried to intervene, he poked her too, causing a similar minor injury. In police work, information is everything. Though this is a far cry from an actual stabbing, it is still a serious matter that can easily escalate to something more dangerous. The use of a knife in this manner could without doubt be articulated as a two-count felony domestic assault. The boy could be arrested, statements could be taken, and the knife could be collected as evidence. A detective and a prosecutor could successfully make a case against this kid.

However, I have met this mother before. Her 17-year-old son has a mental problem. She says that when he does not take his medication, he behaves violently. In the past, I have helped her take him to the hospital emergency room to be petitioned to the mental ward. She has the option of pressing criminal charges against her son or trying again to get him help. Although therapy hasn't helped him so far, she knows that in jail he will have even less of a chance to get help for his mental illness.

America's jails are filled with mentally ill people who don't have access to quality treatment. For families of mentally ill people in an impoverished environment who repeatedly transport loved ones in and out of mental wards, this makes the decision more difficult. More and more, I find that the mental ward, like other forms of social intervention, is yet another revolving door without solutions. From a police standpoint, the mental ward is at the very least a means of temporarily separating dangerous people from society. This is primarily what police officers are asked to do—solve the problem for the moment.

Though police officers are obviously not trained mental health professionals, the nature of our work dictates that we use our experience to gather information, make observations and articulate them in the form of decisions.

The issue of police officer accountability greatly impacts the need to make the best decision possible to temporarily separate dangerous people from society. The knowledge that I will be held responsible for the welfare or the actions of a mentally ill person I might leave on the streets means that I am not only protecting society and the mentally ill person, but I am also indirectly protecting my livelihood.

Through experience, I have found that some of the classic signs of mental illness are: talking to oneself; wearing the same clothes or failing to eat for days at a time; failing to bathe or groom; preoccupation with homicide, suicide, devil-worship; resorting to unprovoked violence.

In this case, the mother tells me her son has been expelled from every school in the city. He terrorizes teachers and fellow students. The boy has begun drinking and using drugs. As always, I try to imagine a positive outcome in every situation. Sadly, another trip to the mental ward is the pinnacle of success.

In another unrelated case, a black mother calls the police about her 14-year-old son. He has grabbed the mother by her collar and assaulted her. The boy stands six feet, four inches and weighs 180 pounds. He towers over his mother. Her eyes are filled with tears. She says his attack was unprovoked. When I try to talk to him, he smiles an evil smile, never initially looking directly at me. When he does decide to look at me, his eyes remind me of Jack Nicholson in the movie, *The Shining*. "Here's Johnny!" I keep thinking. The mother says she has never seen her son like this. I personally have never seen a child capable of such a cold menacing stare. It is almost as if he can look through me.

After handcuffing him and transporting him to the hospital, I begin to avoid looking this kid in the eye because his stare is so evil. I sit with the mother as he is processed for the mental ward. The boy looks off into the distance and mumbles to himself with his fists clenched. He smiles the evil smile several more times and continues mumbling to himself. Finally, the boy is taken to a room and ordered to remove his clothing. When he refuses, hospital security guards rush in and strip the boy of his clothes and place him in four-point restraints.

My job is done. It is now the end of my shift, but for the mother and this child, this is their first experience with the mental ward. Will it be the solution to their problems or the start of many new problems to come? Only time will tell.

TWENTY-SIX

Mom Sets Me Straight

WE RESPOND to a call about a juvenile shoplifter and find a 13-year-old black boy who has stolen a $3 box of bandages. When I ask the boy why he would steal bandages, he shows me a bite mark on his right arm he received from the family dog.

When I ask the boy about his mom, he says she is home sick with the flu. When I ask about his father, he begins to cry and states that he doesn't have one. The lack of a father in the black family is always an emotional subject. It is almost a foregone conclusion that black children in trouble with the law do not have a relationship with their father or any father figure. When I ask about the father, the negative reactions vary from anger and cursing, to an uncaring, unemotional response, to tears. It is obvious that missing fathers leave a void in these children's lives and hearts.

When I call the boy's mother and tell her what he has done, her first reaction is, "Put him in jail!" I am appalled at her attitude. The boy doesn't have an arrest record. Why would she make such a statement?

My partner and I drive the boy home. I tell the mother my thoughts about her statement, and she gives me an earful. She is appalled that I think that she should be grateful that her son is not dead or in jail. She wants more than just a warm body for a son. He is kicked out of school every other week for one thing or another. He doesn't like to go to school because she can't afford name-brand clothing for him. He is the oldest of her five children. She doesn't have any problems with the other four. She is ready to cut her losses with this child for fear that he may contaminate the good children. She is ready to turn the boy over to the state.

After I talk with her, I better understand her frustration. This mother is hardworking. She acknowledges her son's struggle with not having a father, but she doesn't accept excuses for failure. I came to this woman's home to set her straight, but instead I am the one who learns a lesson. I admire her for it, and challenge her son to step up to his mother's expectation.

I will never again suggest to a black mother that she should be satisfied that her son isn't dead or in prison.

As I leave the small home in this predominately poor black neighborhood, I notice words on a small dusty unsigned plaque that hangs on the wall. It best sums up my experience with this family: *"Your life is a gift from God. What you make of it is a gift to God."*

TWENTY-SEVEN

No Room at the Shelter

DOMESTIC VIOLENCE seems to be the most common problem facing African-American women, and it shows itself in many forms. My partner and I are dispatched to a drugstore to assist a victim of domestic violence. We find a terrified woman hiding in a restroom. Police response is slow and she had been waiting there for more than two hours.

When my partner and I arrive, she is still crying and so terrorized that she is afraid to return to her home. She says her husband began attacking her after he stayed awake all night smoking crack cocaine. He grabbed her by her hair several times, slamming her to the floor. He threatened to kill her, but she broke free before he could. She escaped by running to a nearby drug store in bare feet. We take her to a shelter and complete the report. We attempt to locate and arrest her husband without success.

The following day my partner and I respond to a call to assist a woman who wants to remove some personal items from her home. Upon meeting with the woman, we find that she has been raped and beaten by her boyfriend the day before. She has three children, has just recently moved, is unemployed, and is now homeless. The shelters in Flint are all full. She will need to drive her family 50 miles to the next shelter with vacancies. Her small children are just beginning to adjust to a new school. Now they are forced to move again.

TWENTY-EIGHT

Daughter Against Mother

DISPATCH INFORMS my partner and me of a call for domestic violence. Upon reaching the scene, we find a 19-year-old black girl with several large scratches across her face. While holding her 4-month-old daughter, she tells me her mother attacked her because of some meaningless hearsay passed among family members. During the attack the mother pushed her off the front porch as she held the baby, but other than the scratches, no one is hurt.

The mother left the house before my partner and I arrive. The daughter files a complaint against her. The grandmother, with whom they both live, is at her wits end. She witnessed her daughter push her granddaughter off the porch. Her daughter is 35, addicted to cocaine and unemployed. The granddaughter is also unemployed. The grandmother tells me she has 10 grandchildren. Most of them seem to be running in and out of the home as we speak. Four generations of family live in this house, with no grandfathers, fathers, or husbands present. Just women and children.

Hours later we are dispatched to the house again because the mother has returned and is arguing with her daughter. When we arrive, we are forced by departmental policy to arrest her on the earlier complaint filed against her.

This time a small gathering of family members are upset with the 19-year-old for pressing charges against her mother. They try to convince her that she is wrong, but she sticks to her guns. While en route to the station, the mother tells us her daughter and her boyfriend are selling drugs from the home. She vows to get even by putting an end to the operation.

While booking the mother, we find she has two additional warrants for her arrest. Statistically, it is a good day—three arrests in one person—but realistically, the arrest is only a temporary solution. The mother will spend 20 hours in county jail in a cooling off period, but she will return to the streets the following day, an unemployed addict with a dysfunctional family.

Later, in another similar case, my partner and I are dispatched on a call about a woman with a knife. We arrive and find a 22-year-old black woman who says that her 47-year-old mother became angry with her because she refused to give her money for a fifth of vodka. The mother punched her in the back with a closed fist, grabbed her by the collar with one hand while holding a knife in the other, and threatened to kill her. The daughter broke free and ran from the apartment leaving behind her two small children who watched the incident.

The daughter has just gotten out of a shelter with her children and came to live with her mother the week before. The mother is a crack addict and an alcoholic.

She has a history of violence with knives. She spent 15 months in prison for manslaughter after stabbing to death a boyfriend who she says beat her every weekend.

The mother denies grabbing a knife and says that they only argued and tussled a little. She further states that the daughter likes to use her ex-con status against her whenever she can. In short, she claims the daughter has set her up. The animosity and disrespect between them is obvious. They call each other "bitch" and "whore" with the ease that most people say good morning. If my partner and I leave them together, one will certainly hurt the other. Since the daughter is the caller, and she insists on filing a complaint against her mother, we have little choice but to arrest the mother on a felony domestic charge. The daughter states that she is preparing to move as we speak. If this is true, it would be the only other solution to the problem. It is what I would like to have happen, since I can't be 100 percent sure the daughter isn't lying about the knife.

Absent the knife, it is just a tussle and I wouldn't have good cause to arrest either party. All things considered, I must arrest the mother and place her in jail for the 20-hour cooling-off period.

Later, since the daughter is homeless, detectives don't have a way of contacting her to follow through with prosecution. This will be about as far as the case will go.

TWENTY-NINE

Faces of the Black Man

THE DAY after I take a call at a homicide scene, I take a vacation day. I am anxious, hyped up, wound up. Working the streets, having to be aware and observant, and detecting and deciphering meaning from everything at all times heightens the senses and makes it difficult for a police officer to adjust to the slow nature of home life.

By 10 p.m., I am able to relax only after having a beer and watching an episode of *Sanford and Son*. I feel a sense of strong cultural connection to the characters of Fred, Shady Grady, Leroy, Slick Skillet, Bubba and Lamont. They are men, real black men, having fun, dancing, laughing, drinking, as they celebrate the death of a friend. They have a bond and sense of who they are. They talk about the old dances they once did, the places they once went, and the people they once knew. I think about how those men are missing from the black cultural landscape today.

The old-timers. The middle-aged men, who have a keen sense of style, taste, wit and humor. The men who are employed, who walk upright and carry an uncompromising sense of respect and dignity. These were the men most often seen and heard in barbershops, telling various stories in the 1970s. The death of the industrial revolution, the introduction of crack cocaine, and the war on drugs have destroyed this class of black men. It's a shame now that they can only be seen on television.

Nowadays, too many of the few middle-aged black men visible on the streets of the black community are broken and bent-over vagrants, begging, walking with canes, or sitting in wheel chairs. Many of today's black men, ages 20-40, are locked away. The most prominent image in today's black culture is the black male, late teens to early 20s. He is both the victim, dying in a drive-by shooting, and the suspect, doing prison time for committing the shootings.

He is the face on the package of hip-hop culture that more often than not sends negative messages of sex, violence and materialism to mainstream America. The young people of America are obsessed with him. They both love and hate his dark skin, his braids, his jewelry, and his sagging clothes. They try to imitate his walk, his talk, his style. The police like to engage him because he is black and male, and therefore suspicious, even when there is nothing to be suspicious about. His pockets are searched. He is detained while walking or driving. He is chased most times because he runs. He runs most times because he knows the police will chase. But rarely do they find anything. It is just a game of chase between black men and the police. It has gone on for centuries, and it probably will never end.

THIRTY

Sons of Crack

MY PARTNER and I are dispatched to a breaking and entering in progress. It is the same house where the double shooting of two young black men took place many months ago. A memorial for the murdered men, consisting of several helium balloons and stuffed animals tied to a stop sign, has been created. This is a tradition born into black culture by the repeated violent deaths of young black people. Memorials like these exist on many street corners on the predominantly black north side of Flint.

The poor white family who lived here moved immediately after the other murders. They were the only white family in the neighborhood. Their 17-year-old daughter already had one black baby and was pregnant with a second. As it turns out, the father of the second child is one of the black male murder victims.

I cover the front of the house, as two other officers enter from the back. I hear voices inside. I see lights on. Suddenly, I hear the officers yelling at people to get down on the floor. The situation is quickly under control. I join the officers inside, where they have four black male suspects in handcuffs, sprawled face down across the floor. The youngest is 14 years old, and the oldest is 22. Another 22-year-old enters the house, not realizing we are here. We arrest the five of them and take them to the station to be booked. Since the city is officially in a state of financial emergency under receivership by the state of Michigan, our city jail has been closed. The county jail will only take violent offenders. These guys will not go to jail on this night, but they will go to the station to be booked and released.

Personnel shortages prolong the booking process. This type of waiting causes officers to spend more time with people we arrest. If rapport develops, the conversation can be educational. The more we understand the people we police, the better equipped we are to deal with them. It is my observation that some police officers are not that far removed from the lifestyles of the people they police. If they are too far removed from street life, they won't be able to relate. Yet, if they are too close to the streets, they will be ineffective.

A generation separates me from the youngest black men I have just arrested. Because we are all black males, I like to think I am on a fast-track to understanding them, but the more we talk, the more I realize my assumption is a poor one.

The 14- and 16-year-olds have both been shot in previous incidents. I have never been shot and have never known anyone close to me who has. When I was their age, I didn't expect a kid to have possession of a gun. The 14-year-old has been lodged in a juvenile detention center because he was a runaway. At his age, I never knew anyone who had run away from home, and I never knew any child who had been locked away in a detention center.

They further explain a major difference in their generation and mine. "Our mothers are on crack. They don't raise us like back in the day when parents whupped their kids and neighbors even could whup you. Our mothers don't care. They sell dope out of the house. I've been around dope and alcohol since I was four years old. We raise ourselves, and we don't have no hope. We don't see no way out but death. We see death as just another gift from God."

The mother of the 16-year-old cannot be found.

The following day, I am dispatched to another unrelated call for a domestic dispute between a black mother and her 22-year-old son. They are both addicted to cocaine and unemployed. The son is an ex-con who lives in the basement with his white girlfriend and her two children. She is also unemployed. The mother receives money for caring for two handicapped family members who also live in the small crowded home.

The living arrangements cause tensions, but the feud between mother and son runs deep.

"She's been getting high since I was about four or five," he says. "Now that I'm an addict too, she's mad because she sees herself in me. When I'm dealing drugs and giving her drugs and money, she's happy, but now that I'm hooked too, it ain't enough to go around. She didn't raise me. These streets raised me. Everybody I knew in this neighborhood had a mama on crack. Our mamas didn't raise us. We all raised each other."

We take him to a family member's home.

When I grew up, it seemed that every child I knew at least had a mother they could depend on. In my generation, Mother was everything to the black family. With so many fathers gone, Mother was the most honorable image kids clung to. It hurts me to see that so many young black men are unable to speak favorably of either parent. In my mind, this essentially makes them orphans. All they have to depend on is themselves and the streets.

I realize the hardships of my life at their ages do not begin to compare with theirs. How much do we really have in common? Who am I to give them lip service about how to change their lives when I don't understand life as they live it?

THIRTY-ONE

What Did I do Wrong?

MY PARTNER and I respond to a call about a young black man with a gun. Dispatch further states that the man is wearing a black Oakland Raiders jacket. When we arrive, we find a man, who fills the description, standing on the porch. A group of five black males are standing in front of the house. Two of them have pit bulls. As we approach our suspect, he runs inside the house, while the other men slowly scatter. My partner runs in after the suspect and catches him and brings him outside as I watch the other men. The suspect is carrying a .45 caliber handgun and a bag of marijuana. He is 18 years old, selling drugs, he says, to support his 1-year-old daughter.

"Why ya'll bothering me?" he asks. "It ain't like I'm killin' or robbin' nobody. I carry this gun for protection. You know you cain't trus' niggas out here on these streets."

That he honestly doesn't see anything wrong with carrying a loaded gun and selling drugs speaks to the mindset of his generation. I could question why young black men like him don't seek a legitimate means to earn a living. That might be naïve considering that many like him have never seen people operate in socially legitimate ways. When everyone close to him is either in prison or somehow entangled in the criminal justice system, on welfare, selling drugs, dropped out of school or murdered young, his sense of what is legitimate becomes skewed.

However, the law will never take into account the social circumstances of this young black man, and will never miss an opportunity to hold him responsible for his actions. He is already on probation, and he now faces three new felony charges of carrying a concealed weapon, possession with intent to deliver marijuana, and possession of a firearm with an obliterated serial number.

Where does an 18-year-old kid get a large sack of marijuana to sell and a loaded .45 caliber handgun with the serial number scratched off? It really doesn't matter to the system as long as he is caught with it and justice has been served.

THIRTY-TWO

My Own Father

WE ARE dispatched to a domestic dispute on a certain street just a couple blocks from where I spent my teenage years. My mother still lives a few blocks away. I recall the many times I walked to the corner store in the late '70s and early '80s. The winos and panhandlers were there, begging for loose change to buy cheap liquor, but they were harmless and most times hospitable in their own way. Now, crack cocaine has turned the corner store into a hotbed of illegal activity.

Rarely if ever are the local stores owned by blacks. The people who own them frequently exploit the black community in numerous ways. They sell single cigarettes at high prices, sell liquor to the already addicted and homeless, and charge high prices for household items such as baby formula, diapers and low-quality food items. Those who buy are people without transportation to the traditional super markets that have now relocated away from the inner-city community.

The party stores, with the words *LIQUOR, LOTTO, COLDEST BEER IN TOWN, FOOD STAMPS GLADLY ACCEPTED, PAGERS AND CELL PHONES,* plastered in huge letters on their sides are often the fastest growing businesses in poor black communities. Politically, very little is done to control the expansion of these stores in urban areas, while suburban communities limit the number of these types of stores that can exist in a square-mile area.

As my partner and I sit on the street near the party store, we talk with the black woman who called us out. She has had an argument with her black alcoholic boyfriend. As we speak to her, he rides down the sidewalk on a bicycle, highly intoxicated, wobbling. He loses control and rides into the street toward oncoming traffic and is nearly struck by a car. Finally he wobbles out of sight, and the woman is satisfied that he is gone.

Moments later, I see another figure, a tall older black male walking with a three pronged walker in one hand. He looks like a homeless person. He stops at an open gate and gently closes it because it is blocking the sidewalk, then continues walking toward us. As the figure gets closer, I recognize him to be my biological father with whom I haven't had a relationship since I was 7 or 8 years old. Ashamed at the sight of him, I abruptly end the conversation with the woman and drive away. I am too embarrassed to speak to him, or to explain to my partner that he is my father. If we were to come face to face, what would either of us say?

THIRTY-THREE

Poetic Justice

AFTER SIX days off work, I am refreshed and ready to
go. My first call is for a stabbing in the block where 14
abandoned houses exist.

I arrive at the home with two other officers. We find
a black family of alcoholics who have been drinking
heavily and arguing. Their brother has recently died.
The funeral is the following day, and tensions are high.
One man is hyper-verbal and equally hyperactive, while
another sits on the porch and cries aloud every so often.
After making his rounds of yelling and agitating
everyone, including the officers at the scene, the hyper
man hugs the crying man and states at the top of his
voice, "I'm here for you, man," at which time the crying
man cries even louder.

As I talk to this alcoholic family, I get yet another
lesson. The story is that another brother had grabbed a
large kitchen knife and began threatening to kill
everyone in the house. He has already struck his sister
in the face five times with a closed fist and choked her
until another drunken family member pulled him off.

After making death threats to his sister, he raised the knife at her and began charging. Family members restrained him again. During the struggle, the knife accidentally cut another woman. She is transported to the hospital by ambulance.

After sorting out these details, the assaulted sister makes a complaint for felonious assault domestic against her brother. We arrest the brother and take him away, where he will spend at least 20 hours in county jail as a "cooling off period." It will be up to his sister to prosecute. Since she is not seriously injured, the detectives will drop the case if she doesn't show interest.

Chances are, the worst thing that will happen to this man is that he will miss his brother's funeral. Maybe, in some strange way, that will be a kind of poetic justice.

Another officer at the scene says, "I wish I had a video camera. This is Flint, Michigan. Nobody would believe this."

I share the sentiments of this officer. Much of what the police experience goes unseen by the general public, and we often find it difficult to explain to the public. The average working citizens in any community live routine lives that take them to the same daily place of employment. However, the police officer is called into places an average citizen has no reason to go, to witness things they will never see. For 26 years of my life, I lived as a civilian and never saw the city the way I see it now. Before I became an officer, I thought I really knew my hometown.

THIRTY-FOUR

History Lost

Working alone today, I take a call for a breaking and entering report on the west side of town, which was once affluent but is now in slow decline. I meet with a 40-year-old black man, who owns the vacant home. He lives an hour away, so it is difficult to keep a close eye on the place. The break-in has even slipped past the watchful eye of concerned neighbors.

The man who grew up in the neighborhood is now an automotive company executive. He is divorced. Though he does not want to sell the home, which is still in good repair and fully furnished, he feels forced to consider it. Renting it out, he feels, would be about the same as, or worse than, being burglarized these days.

To gain entry, the burglars broke out the large dining room windows. They ransacked the place, but didn't take anything this time. Chances are they will return later. They left the side door open when they exited.

This is how the man found his house when he arrived. For now, he will board up the home. This will create an eyesore, and begin yet another phase of decline in this predominately black neighborhood.

On the surface, it appears that the black people, who in the late 1960s fought for open housing to be able to purchase homes in areas like these, are now responsible for destroying the neighborhood. However, more than likely, the younger black people are responsible for destroying the property. They don't have appreciation for the struggles of the previous generations that fought for their right to live in the neighborhood. The whites, of course, have now moved away, and even black professionals like this man see no advantage to living in the city limits when they can afford to do otherwise.

"I love Flint. It's my home town," the man states, "but I could never come back here to live. It's too negative." Expressing his disgust at the young blacks whom he suspects are responsible for the break-in, he says, "I know it's those little 'nigglets.' I know it's them. I can't stand them."

THIRTY-FIVE

Tears of a Young Father

UPON RESPONDING to a call for domestic violence in a housing project, I meet a young black man, age 21. He and his girlfriend have a 2-year-old child and she is expecting a second child. They are both unemployed. The young man doesn't live with his girlfriend but visits everyday. He has other family members who live in the complex, but no place of his own. He is hurt because he does not understand his girlfriend's mood swings caused by her pregnancy. He hurts also because she uses their children against him during these moments.

He recalls how his mother suffered domestic violence and was left alone to raise him in poverty. With tears now rolling down his face and his right hand placed over his heart, he vows before me never to do anything to hurt his children. His sincerity makes me want to help him find a job. I offer help and take his number. As a police officer, I am sure I can talk some employer into giving this young man a chance to provide something for his children. As a black police officer working in the poor black community, I figure it is the least I can do. Though his girlfriend has called the police on him, I find that his only crime is that he cares about his children and is just not equipped to provide for them.

He hugs and thanks me. I call him some days later, but the number is disconnected. I think maybe I should go back to his girlfriend's apartment to find him, but I am undecided about how much I should reach out. I haven't forgotten him. If I never see him again, I can only hope he will have found his way.

THIRTY-SIX

Veterans of Wars, Foreign and Domestic

A MOTHER has reported that her son called her and said his father is holding him at gun point. The story sounds suspicious, because nobody uses the phone when held at gun point. Still, we must respond and sort out the details. I find that most of my work as a police officer involves making sense of the senselessness. However, beneath all seemingly senseless things rests a reason.

Upon arriving, we speak to the father, who turns out to be a Vietnam veteran. He is 54, and slightly disabled. He walks with a limp, but this doesn't stop him from physically disciplining his 15-year-old son for stealing $300 from him. The father has custody of the child because the mother is a crack addict. His son also has attention deficit disorder for which he receives disability payments. I find that an increasing amount of African-American adults and children receive payments for mental and physical disabilities.

The son admits to falsely stating that his father held a gun against him to provoke his mother to action.

The father states that he is an Agent Orange victim. He is struggling with the federal government over his disability payments and struggling with a lying, stealing child.

"I spent 13 months and one day killing babies for my country and this is what I get," he says.

The son takes some clothing and leaves with his mother who has already demonstrated that she can't care for him.

In an unrelated case, I am dispatched to a call on an argument between a mother and her adult son. The son is 21. He is military veteran of the Gulf War. He has been out of the military only one month. His mother is a drug addict and has spent all his savings. He is depressed. His mother says he needs mental help and she wants him to leave her home. Being a military veteran, I try to talk positively to him. I know that the adjustment from being a soldier to being a civilian is a difficult one. I spent seven years in the Army directly out of high school. After leaving the military, I spent seven more years trying to become a civilian again. Then I found myself back in uniform.

I watch the dejected young man sit on his mother's porch in the middle of winter. His mother has now literally closed the door on him as he sits there. Across the street sit several abandoned houses. Flint has very few, if any, positive opportunities to offer a young black military veteran with no family support. Even civil service jobs, such as a police work, fire fighting or in sanitation, are no longer available to him as this city has been forced to lay off the people holding many of these positions.

He decides to leave. As he drives away in his car, I can't help but think he has something good to offer the world, but he may never find it. The military was likely his only opportunity to get off the streets, but war drove him away from a military career. Now another war awaits him in the streets of Flint, and he seems destined to lose it.

THIRTY-SEVEN

Misery Loves Company

A VIOLENT woman is reported to be destroying the home and breaking things. Upon arriving, I find that it is a domestic dispute involving a black couple who have become very familiar to me over the course of my career. In fact, they are perhaps the most difficult and yet interesting couple I have ever dealt with during my time in the department.

They are both crack addicts. They are both physically and verbally abusive to each other. Their two children are constantly exposed to their antics. The way they curse and badmouth each other even in my presence makes it impossible for me to understand how either of them can be with the other. It is said that misery loves company. Whenever I encounter this couple, I always wonder which one of them is the company. Yin and Yang.

On this day, the husband claims his wife has broken a dinner plate on the living room floor. I see a broken plate in one corner of the living room, but breaking dishes is no crime. Besides, the real issue here is not about dishes. As I talk to them, I find that the real problem is that they have smoked away the money for household expenses in their crack pipes. After the money is gone, the fighting begins. The consequences of their actions set in. When the high is gone, the cupboards and refrigerator are bare and the water and electricity have been turned off.

In the midst of it all, they must face their two daughters. The oldest is 12 and the youngest is 5. Both of them seem to have adjusted to their highly abnormal family life. Neither seems outwardly upset by circumstances that I believe would devastate most children. In particular, the youngest child seems to have developed a high level of intelligence despite the circumstances. She sits and plays a hand-held computer game on which she can identify all 50 states. She shows my partner and me brilliant crayon drawings and offers to draw one for us.

The most amazing thing about this child is that she speaks perfect English in a household where curse words and street slang appear to be the norm. How can a child living under these conditions develop like this?

I notify Children's Protective Services of the circumstances. When they arrive, the couple are still arguing and blaming each other. Children's Protective Services takes a report, but doesn't offer any immediate action. My partner and I clear the call without the sense that we have made any sort of impact at all. Misery and company remain together.

THIRTY-EIGHT

All in a Day's Work

WE ANSWER a call for trouble with a child, and we find a young black couple, who have taken on the challenge of trying to raise the woman's 13-year-old nephew. The boy has lived with them only five days and has already assaulted and cursed his aunt. He also threatens to assault other members of the family. Attempts to discipline him only set him off worse. They are at a loss as to how to deal with him.

The boy is carrying a lot of emotional baggage. He is on probation for rape and carrying a concealed weapon. He is also facing expulsion from the Flint schools on the weapons charge. His mother died of AIDS in 1998, and he has never known his father, who is in prison. Additionally, the boy has been diagnosed with mental problems and is on medication. He hasn't had his medication since living with this family. He left it where he last lived with another family member. Because of a disagreement between the two households, the previous family refuses to pass along the child's medication to his new family.

The man of the house at the boy's new home collects disability for a multitude of ailments. He states that he has just received a $28,000 back payment check for disability. He is 40, and appears on the surface to be a physically healthy person. However, he doesn't exhibit the patience or the willingness needed to help the boy with his problems. He sits in a small room on a bare mattress drinking a 40-ounce beer and smoking cigarettes. He openly states that he does not want the boy here and that if his girlfriend wants to keep him she will be on her own.

The girlfriend is unemployed. She cries because she doesn't want to give up on her dead sister's child, but like her boyfriend, she doesn't really seem up to the task. She makes it clear that if she has to choose between her boyfriend and the child, the child will be the odd man out.

The house is infested with roaches. My partner keeps slapping his legs and brushing himself off as we stand talking to the family. Finally we decide to take the child to the hospital for emergency mental health care. The family doesn't have a car. This is an additional burden on us as police officers because our cruiser again becomes a taxi service for the child, his older sister, and his aunt. The hospital will provide them with a voucher for a taxi to get home. The lives of many black families I meet are heavily dependent on some type of agency intervention.

At the hospital, the aunt will need to file a petition for the boy to receive a mental evaluation. Hopefully he will be institutionalized long enough to at least get back on his medication. At any rate, it is only a short-term solution. In a day or two he will be released. Under the circumstances, it is doubtful he will have a stable family environment to return to, and even if this family decides to keep him, it is doubtful they can really help him. With so much uncertainty and so many problems, his chances for success over the long term seem extremely limited. He seems destined to be institutionalized in one way or another. As shameful as it is, this might be the best thing that can happen to him.

THIRTY-NINE

My Old Neighborhood

I RECEIVE a call to assist a special unit in a raid of an illegal after-hours joint. It is located in a predominately black part of town where I lived during my teen years until I graduated high school and joined the military. As a young teen, I walked past this place hundreds of times. My mother still lives just two blocks from here. I recall that in the mid to late '70s, several of what adults called "gambling joints" were located on the north end of this old street.

An uncle of mine loved gambling and occasionally would be caught in raids, which at the most would result in him spending a few hours at the police station. Whenever he failed to make it home before daylight, we all knew he had been caught in a raid. Most times, word would hit the street that there had been a raid at so-and-so's. Someone would come to my aunt's home and let her know that her husband was caught in it. He would return home a few hours later with no explanation or excitement. It was just normal.

Now, decades later, I find myself standing in one such joint for the first time in my life. About 20 people are inside, most of them senior citizens, and all of them black. In the room are pool tables and makeshift games of chance. A ghetto version of a casino. Playing cards line every table. Large lights hang from the ceiling in the smoke-filled room, some of them circular others rectangular. A sign on the wall states: *No guns or drugs allowed!* But of course guns and drugs are here. About five of the people are arrested for possession of both, and a substantial amount of money is seized.

The sergeant in charge of the raid makes the following speech to the remaining people: "You all are free to go. You are free to even stay here if you wish. You know you are not supposed to be gambling, but at least wait until we get out of the door before you start again." In other words, the powers that be have no interest in shutting down illegal gambling joints in the black community. They are only interested in making the occasional raid that results in a few small drug and weapons arrests. Then again, we have seized money. That's more than likely the reason illegal gambling joints in poor black communities will never be shut down.

FORTY

Success is Hard to Find

We arrive at an apartment complex in a historical district near downtown Flint where dispatch has told us a domestic assault is in progress. The neighborhood has an odd mix of large classic housing structures in various stages of decline and renovation. Not far away are several group homes, which house mentally ill adults, the homeless, and drug addicts. Not very many of these people own cars, so the foot traffic is heavy.

As we search for the apartment number, we observe a very dark black woman wearing dreadlocks and a tattered beige overcoat. She is walking in the courtyard of the apartment complex. She points us in the direction of the disturbance without speaking a word and disappears into the darkness.

We take her cue without a verbal response. As we reach the top of a small set of winding cement stairs, we hear the screams of a woman coming from inside the apartment. The door is partially open. With our guns drawn, we immediately go inside. As we enter, I notice a large hole in the drywall directly in front of us.

The apartment is dark. The screams are coming from a room to the rear left of the apartment.

My partner heads in the direction of the screams as I turn right to check the living room and kitchen to be sure no one is hiding there. As I search, I can hear the intensity of my partner's voice as he reaches a closed door from which the screams continue to come. The mix of his voice, the screams, and the loud booming noises of his foot striking that door heightens the tension.

Unable to get the door open, he threatens to shoot through it. The woman is still screaming. Not knowing how this might turn out, I call for additional backup and an ambulance. I am certain this is a hostage situation in which someone might get hurt. I have never handled a hostage situation before and my partner has less time on the department than I have. Police work is largely about experience; the most experienced officer on scene generally makes command decisions.

Within seconds of my request, I can hear the faint sounds of sirens coming toward us from all directions. There is a certain security in knowing that backup is on its way, yet sheer numbers of officers alone can't reveal what is happening on the other side of that door.

When I reach my partner, we both begin kicking the door, not knowing what we might find on the other side. Just a day before, a Flint police officer had survived being shot in the chest on a traffic stop. His vest stopped the bullet. His shooting shortly followed the murder of two Detroit officers who were also on a traffic stop. Now, my partner and I are risking our lives without fully acknowledging that our lives may be in jeopardy. We are reacting to save a life, not thinking about our own. We stand before that door, kicking it, using our weight to strike it with our shoulders until it opens. At that instant, a person with a gun on the other side could easily kill us both.

We finally get the door open enough to get inside. We find a black female victim lying on the floor in a pile of dirty clothing. After searching under the bed and in the closet we realize she is alone. She has been holding a huge dresser against the door because she thinks we are the boyfriend who has just beaten her. With the dresser now lying across the bottom part of her legs, where it fell when we pushed the door, she lies there physically exhausted, out of breath and motionless from her effort to keep us out of the room.

Just as we realize there is no immediate threat, the other officers begin arriving on scene. Setting the dresser upright, we help the woman from the floor and into the living room, where she sits in a chair, still trying to catch her breath from the ordeal. She gives us the story. Her boyfriend is jealous of her children. Because of substance abuse, she has lost her children to the state but is in the process of trying to get her life together to convince the authorities to return them. Her boyfriend is threatened by her desire to better her life. He wants her to stay addicted and childless so that he can dominate her life, but she is resistant. The hole in the drywall was made when her boyfriend drove her head through it, and she now has several large swellings.

Because of the city's financial crisis, we no longer have a city ambulance service. Citizens are dependent upon several suburban ambulance companies, which respond from miles away and charge high fees. The response time is slow. It seems that everyone has found a way to make a profit from the suffering of poor black people. In this case, it is literally 20 minutes or more before the ambulance arrives. Luckily, the woman is not critically injured. The ambulance crew checks her over and tries to convince her to go to the hospital, but she refuses. In the end, none of us can do anything but file reports. The ambulance crew leaves after a few minutes. My partner and I attempt to find the woman's boyfriend without success. Success, it seems, is hard to find in this business.

FORTY-ONE

Ghost of America's Conscience

WE RESPOND to a call at an intersection of Martin Luther King Jr. Boulevard for unknown trouble. The street runs north from the Flint River through the center of the city. It is literally a spine to which may poor black communities are attached.

On this day, the sun shines brightly with not a cloud in the sky. This, I equate with happiness, yet a certain sad imperfection lingers beneath the perfect blue skies on King Boulevard. I find this contrast further defined by the many old apartment buildings that have been transformed into residential drug treatment facilities and group homes for the mentally ill. The so-called vagrants, beggars and panhandlers are here. Some stand at bus stops while others sit waiting for something other than the bus.

Through my constant interaction with people, my senses are greatly developed. At times, I can literally feel the good and bad energy. The energy that moves inside me is negative as I continue patrolling past a short section of blighted commercial structures on my left. Just past the structures sits a house surrounded by a large wooden fence. It looks like a military fort. A mentally ill woman lives here. She has painted various messages in large white letters on the fence and windows: *THIS HOUSE IS UNDER ILLEGAL GOVERNMENT SURVEILLANCE. POLICE BEAT PEOPLE. KILLER COPS. COURT FRAUD. KISS MY ASS. MIND YOUR OWN BUSINESS. FRADULENT GODS. FAKE CHURCHES.* She has also written the names of the police officers in our department who have transported her to the mental ward on various occasions. My name is not yet there.

To my right is one of many liquor stores. Painted on the wall of an abandoned structure next to it are the images of Martin Luther King Jr. and Malcolm X side by side. Why must a street plagued with vice be named after Dr. King? I know this is not the dream he had for America. I wonder how many streets are named after Dr. King in white communities in this country and if his image graces any buildings there. America has minimized his dream. As I look at the painting, I am reminded of how one group of Michigan citizens is fighting to outlaw Affirmative Action. I think a visit to King Boulevard will shake their consciousness.

Finally, I reach my destination. I find a black man wearing all white, standing in front of his small apartment. His head is shaved and his beard is neatly trimmed. He is intoxicated and he holds a glass of wine. He takes on a divine appearance as the sun shines on his garments. *Black Jesus* pops into my mind. I have encountered this man many times. He is an unemployed ex-con on medication for mental illness. On previous occasions, he has shared with me several news articles written about him in various newspapers across the country. Some refer to him as a prison intellectual who was many times punished by the prison system for being outspoken about the realities of prison life. He has published articles on prison life and wrote book reviews for several newspapers. I know this man is as intelligent, if not more so than many so-called "important" people from business, religion and politics who have crossed my path.

On this day, he called the police because he is bothered by his surroundings. The drug users and prostitutes constantly knock at his door. He wants them to go away.

"Officer Willingham, I loan these people money," he says. "I give them advice. I try to help them. I try to make my community better, and they knock at my door constantly, 24 hours a day. I'm tired, man. I want all this to go away."

I listen to him and think maybe he doesn't realize that he and they have gone away and this is where they wound up together, on King Boulevard, across the street from the paintings of King and Malcolm X.

For as long as I have known this man, he has always shared with me monologues of his prison experience. His ability to launch into a poetic speech from memory amazes me. As we talk, he does just that:

"When I finally leave prison there will be no turning back for me, no looking over my shoulder for a final glimpse of the misery and degradation I've just abandoned. I have encountered many experiences that I can never forget or forgive. I surrendered my youth to the dungeons of prison society. It's a terrible feeling that a man often gets when he realizes that he's the filth that's been left by the wayside. His fellow countrymen's victorious disposition: 'Yeah, we got him off the streets,' is his hell forever. The days are extraordinarily long and the nights are bitterly lonely. If this is my station in life, I don't want anything to do with it. I have failed. I have lost my task of being worthy of my fellow citizen's respect and consideration. I am always left to deal with this reality in isolation where no one shall see my profound despair. I want to live the life of a man. Responsibility, accountability, credibility and integrity are the call of the day. I accept full responsibility for my crime. I don't place the blame on society's shoulders. However, I do not consider myself a criminal. I reject that name.

"Approximately 25 years ago, I offended society. I was subjugated to a lengthy incarceration of 12-15 years for my so-called wicked iniquities. I am certain that I have received a cruel and unusual punishment for the offense known as armed robbery with a broken, dilapidated BB gun. Theoretically speaking, I have not been rehabilitated. I am not getting constructive treatment that will allow me to become a productive citizen. I have been forgotten. They don't understand that this has made me the real criminal that the bureaucrats and politicians have said I was.

"There are many individuals like myself who have been polluted, contaminated and dehumanized without justification for such foul and treacherous treatment. I have been betrayed and manipulated by some abstract autocratic elements. I have been stripped of my credibility, individuality, and my manhood has been verbally violated. I am expected to act normal in an abnormal environment, to always be agreeable and never questionable. It appears to be an extremely undemocratic expectation. You might wonder if it is the fault of the government that crime is rising. Or is it the fault of parole boards who release animals back onto the streets to victimize the innocent citizen? Or maybe is it the fault of the police officer who preys on the weak and disenfranchised?

"Well, heck, who's to blame for what we see before us, Officer Willingham? I say we all are to blame."

He raises the glass of wine as if to toast his conclusion. I shake his hand as he smiles and nods at me. He seems to feel better because I have listened to him. As I drive away, I can't help but think that more people should hear what he has to say, though I know they never will. Finally, I realize that no matter how hard some may try to erase the legacy of Dr. King and those who walk the streets named for him, they remain the ghosts that haunt the American conscience.

FORTY-TWO

Nine Warrants, No Arrest

A MAN has reported trouble with his wife. We find a highly intoxicated man locked outside of his home during a rainstorm. He tries to convince us that his wife has struck him twice in the face with a closed fist, but neither of us believes him.

After a few thousand conversations with citizens, I have developed what I consider a sixth sense. I find that people generally embellish their version of an event to benefit themselves and discredit others. Some of the key indicators are body language, tone of voice, and the eyes. In this case, I hear certain insincerity in the man's voice. As I investigate further, I find a child in the house who states that the mother has not struck the father.

When I talk to the wife, I find that the real reason for the dispute is that the man has been gone from home for several days. Additionally, he is unemployed and his wife has grown tired of supporting him. The real problem becomes evident very quickly. The man is trying to conceal the fact that he, not his wife, is the problem.

I check his name through L.E.I.N. and find that he has nine arrest warrants for charges such as operating a motor vehicle under the influence, contempt of court, failure to pay income tax, and driving with a suspended license. However, I can't take the man to jail because the city jail is closed.

Warrant arrests, which are based on existing warrants, are great tools for officers. They make easier the job of separating problem people from society and eliminating repeated calls to a single address. However, because of the jail situation, I am unable to make an arrest based only on old warrants. The fact that I do not have a fresh charge on which to arrest the man creates a new problem. I must resort to a tactic that hopefully will compel the man to leave without revealing to him that I do not have legal authority to make him do so. When I advise the man that he is under arrest for existing warrants, his wife and children become hysterical. The man has not long been out of prison. The family does not want him to go back to jail. The man begs my partner and me not to take him to jail. We handcuff him and place him in our cruiser, knowing that we can't lodge him in jail. His family runs out to the cruiser and begs us again not to take him to jail. We tell them that we have no choice. The man has warrants. We are the police. We have a job to do.

After a few moments, we pretend to show compassion for the family. We agree to let him walk to his mother's house, as long as he doesn't return until the next day. Believing that we have given him a break, the man is glad to go to his mother's home. The family is glad that he isn't going to jail. My partner and I are glad that we have creatively found a temporary solution to a problem.

FORTY-THREE

The Vicious Cycle

AN APPARENTLY highly intoxicated man has been seen staggering about a busy intersection. We get his name and address and transport him home so he doesn't get hurt. Though he is drunk out of his mind, he hasn't forgotten where he lives. We briefly speak with his family before letting him out of the cruiser. His family expresses gratitude as we help him to the door.

After dropping the man at home, we stop in the parking lot of a former local elementary school to dump some trash in a receptacle. The school is closed due to a budget crisis and declining enrollment. At its peak in the 1970s, the school once held 1,000 students. When it closed in 2002, it barely held 300.

I read in the newspaper about a local elementary school mobility rate that indicates that of the 529 students starting school there this year, 403 have comings and goings at a rate of 76 percent. A combined study of one classroom with 35 children showed that the children have attended 130 schools and lived in 104 homes. The report catches my attention because I had volunteered in that school in an after-school photography class the year before.

In this predominately black community, people stand on street corners and drink alcohol. On the west side of the school is a liquor store. On the east side of the school, directly across from the main parking lot, sits an abandoned house. Across the lot, on the north side of the school sits a recently closed elementary school building. The closed school building is dilapidated and thought by many to be an unsafe place to educate children. Not long before it closed, a stray bullet had passed through the window of a third grade classroom nearly striking a teacher. Students from this school, together with students from another dilapidated closed school, were consolidated into the school where I once volunteered.

During a portion of the class, I would take walking field trips through the surrounding neighborhood with the students. We would take pictures of the things that made up the neighborhood. I noted then that absolutely no positive messages exist in their environment.

While in the school parking lot, I notice a large cloud of thick black smoke rising from a nearby neighborhood. Driving just east of the school, we find a house engulfed in flames. We notify dispatch and begin evacuating neighbors next door who believe a child is trapped inside the burning home.

Moments later, we find the child, a young teen, walking the streets barefooted. Now he tells us he thinks his father might be trapped inside. The boy had fallen asleep on the couch. He was awakened when his pants caught fire. At that point he saved only himself. There was no time to think of saving anyone else.

Soon the father returns in a panic. He left a hot skillet with grease cooking on the stove. In the time it took him to drive around the corner to a store to buy corn meal and seasonings to fry catfish, he had burned the house down. I try to stop him from approaching the house as firefighters fight the flames. He yells, "I got a son in there!" I assure him that his son has gotten out safely, but he doesn't seem thankful for that. Instead, he goes on about the loss of material things and the fact that he doesn't have insurance. Furthermore, he seems more worried about what his girlfriend will say when she finds that the house is burned down.

The next day I go to the home with my camera and shoot some pictures inside it. I want to get a feel for what it must be like to lose every material thing you own in a matter of minutes. The house is dark and eerie. Sunlight shines through what were windows, giving it an even more ghostly feel. I remember watching the windows explode during the fire.

The living room furniture sits charred on the curb, yet the two bedrooms are still intact. The blankets on the beds are black from the smoke. Clothes are still in one closet. An iron that sits on a nightstand is also black from the fire, as are the light bulbs, which are still in sockets. In the kitchen, melted spice containers still sit on the shelves.

The house was worth no more than $12-15,000 before it burned. Demolition will cost more. When one doesn't have insurance, how does one afford that? When the city is in financial crisis, how can it afford to demolish the house? How long will the house sit unattended? Will it become a new site for illegal activity? In a neighborhood where property values have bottomed out, people are unemployed, schools are closing and crime is high, this is a vicious cycle I'm not sure can be broken.

FORTY-FOUR

Trust Lost

TONIGHT I work alone. My first call is to check the welfare of an elderly woman who has received a death threat. I find the information odd, because the elderly aren't the usual death-threat victims. However, part of an officer's job is to go to the scene, communicate and sort out facts, determine problems, and find solutions. On many occasions, after an officer has gone through this process, he or she can find that the actual nature of the call is something totally different than the initial reason stated by dispatchers.

In this case, I find that the callers are concerned neighbors who found a mentally and physically disabled black woman crawling in the middle of the street. The disabled woman lives across the street from the concerned citizens. They have taken her into their home, but now the question is what to do with her. They state that this is not the first time the woman has been found in the street.

I locate the disabled woman's brother who is legally responsible for her. He states that the woman has gotten out of the home without his knowledge. I sense that the man is not properly equipped to care for his sister.

In police work, a hunch is enough to investigate further. Many times, no set rules are available on how to handle a particular situation. Much is left to the discretion and instinct of the individual officer in the field, facing situations for which he can't possibly have been trained. For me, this moment falls into that category. I look at the man's home. I see that it is unkempt and in disrepair. The yard is filled with trash. If the outside appearance is any indication of what is going on inside, there might be problems. I need to get inside, but I need permission. If I am not tactful, he might become defensive and refuse. Then, I might really need a sergeant to tell me what to do next.

I am patient with him. He is cooperative and eager to explain himself. He tells me his sister became disabled when her former boyfriend poisoned her. Since then, she has been confined to a wheelchair.

Without his knowing it, I contact Social Services and advise them of the situation.

They instruct me to leave the woman with the neighbors who found her. They also ask me to investigate the inside of the man's home for additional signs of neglect. Ironically, without knowing that Social Services has asked me to investigate, the man offers me a chance to look inside his home. He does so with confidence, as if it will prove him a fit caregiver.

However, once I check the home, I find that there is no food or running water. I don't know why he has offered me this chance. Perhaps he was bluffing, thinking that I wouldn't actually check, or maybe he is just really out of touch with the fact that he is unfit to care for his sister.

After informing Social Services of my findings, I am sure they will respond immediately to help the sick woman and relieve the concerned neighbors of the responsibility of caring for her. Instead, I am told it will take hours, possibly until the next morning, before they will respond. At this point, there is nothing more I can do.

I have succeeded in identifying a problem, but I have not succeeded in helping the neighbors who are stuck with the woman. Had they refused to keep the woman, I'm not sure what I would have done next. There is the situation concerning the woman's brother. He seems passive on the surface, but I can't be sure he won't cause problems for the concerned neighbors once I leave. It is yet another risk for neighbors. I could arrest the man for a misdemeanor neglect charge, for which he would only be booked and released in a matter of hours. To do this would not solve the problem. The time I would spend attending to such an arrest means less time I can spend helping the woman. I wish for one decision that would remedy this situation. Sometimes multiple problems are found on one call. Much like a hospital emergency room must triage injuries according to their severity, I must decide which problem is most pressing. Without a doubt, the woman is most important.

Though I am wearing a uniform with a badge attached to my chest, a bulletproof vest, and a loaded 9mm on my hip, I realize that the neighbors in this case are actually the ones "protecting and serving." I can't think of a time on the job when I have felt more inadequate. Morally, I still feel a connection to this call. I do not feel my job is done. I still believe I am responsible for seeing the neighbors through this ordeal. I must leave, but we exchange phone numbers so I can follow their progress.

I check back with the family four hours later between other calls and find that Social Services still has not contacted the family, who have fed and bathed the woman. I call Social Services again. They tell me the adult foster care division has failed to respond to their pages and that no one will respond until 9 a.m. the following morning. Now the neighbors are stuck caring for this woman overnight.

Out of curiosity, I call the neighbors the next morning at 11 a.m. and find that Social Services has informed them that they should not have kept the woman and that they should give her back to her brother if he comes back to get her.

The brother doesn't come back to get her, and the neighbors are still stuck between an uncaring brother and a dysfunctional government agency. I contact Social Services again on this morning and they explain that the system is badly broken. They promise to contact the neighbors immediately, but they are still unable to give a time frame as to when they will respond.

Four days later the neighbors call me. They still have the woman in their home and both Social Services and the woman's brother have failed to call or come by. Though I can't prove it, I would bet this episode is something that only happens in the black community. Not only is the disabled woman a victim, but so are her caring neighbors.

I place yet another call, and I am again informed that the system has failed. On the fifth day, Social Services does finally come to get the woman. Thanks to the neighbors, a woman in need is saved. What is lost, however, is the neighbors' trust in the system. If it ever existed, I doubt now that it can ever be restored.

FORTY-FIVE

Voiceless Victims

THE NIGHT has been busy, but the calls have not been serious until my partner and I are dispatched to the scene of a rape. Because dispatch states that the suspect is still on the scene, another officer who is working alone decides to go with us.

When the three of us arrive in a poor section of the black community, we find the small house filled with extended family. Three sets of adults and three sets of children are living under the same roof. More than 10 people live in this house, and it seems that all of them are trying to tell the story at once. Sorting through the confusion, I find the mother of a 2-year-old girl and separate her from the crowd. She tells me she believes that her 14-year-old nephew has raped her daughter. Before I can take action, I must ask some very tough questions.

"Why do you think your nephew raped your daughter?"

"He had her in the bathroom alone for more than 40 minutes—the whole time the family was looking for her. We thought she had gotten out of the house or that someone had kidnapped her."

"How did you discover that he had been in there with her?"

"I saw him walk out with her after we had been yelling for her."

"What was his reaction when he came out?"

"I asked him what he had been doing in there with her and he just laughed."

"Did you notice anything strange about your daughter when she came out?"

"Yeah, she had something clear on her lips."

"What did it look like to you?"

"Maybe semen."

"What did you do next?"

"I took a towel and wiped her mouth off."

"Where is towel?"

"I put it in the sink."

"Did you check your daughter's vaginal area for any signs of semen?"

"No."

"Why not?"

She shrugs her shoulders as if to say, "I don't know."

"Please do that right now so I can decide whether or not to make an arrest."

On one hand, I am surprised that I have to give such explicit instructions when the mother already suspects that her daughter has been raped. On the other hand, I realize that because of the extended family situation there may be some level of denial. The suspect is her sister's son, which makes it more difficult than if it were a stranger. There would be outrage if the suspect was a stranger. I can see that a part of the mother is hoping it is not true, and this is why she hasn't investigated her daughter's body further. However, she wants justice for her child in case her suspicion has merit, so she called the police, expecting us to find what she did not have the courage to find.

She takes the child into the bathroom and checks her vaginal area as I instruct her and finds what appears to be semen. It is enough for me to make an arrest of the 14-year-old. I take him into custody and call for an ambulance for the 2-year-old. I ride in the ambulance with the 2-year-old, her 4-year-old sister, and both parents. The ambulance crew straps the tiny girl to a stretcher and gives her a small stuffed animal to hold during the ride.

The 2-year-old seems to be a normal child, with pretty brown skin and reddish brown hair pulled into a bushy ponytail that sits tall on the top of her head. She sits quietly and content for most of the ride. When she does talk, it is totally spontaneous, but she does not respond to direct questions. Her mother asks her what happened to her without success. She is basically a voiceless victim. Without physical evidence, there won't be any proof of the crime against her. It will take an examination from a doctor to provide the proof that we need.

Once at the hospital, I advise a social worker of the situation and call a detective as doctors begin the examination. By now, my partner and the other officer have transported the 14-year-old to the station with his mother so that he can be interviewed. The mother of the 14-year-old, who was also at the scene at the time of the arrest lives just two doors from the house we were called to. The boy doesn't live with her. He lives with his grandmother in the house we were called to. The boy doesn't know his father.

The boy is quiet and withdrawn with a clean-cut appearance. If he was standing in a crowd of boys and I was asked to pick one I thought would rape a 2-year-old girl, I would not pick him. Perhaps the person I might pick would not be the least bit capable of rape. Thinking of it that way, I realize there are no set physical profiles of people who commit crimes. Information, especially the suspicions and denials of the family and friends of suspects, is crucial to street-level investigations.

When the doctors complete their examination, the rape is confirmed. Semen is found inside the girl and there are tears to her vagina. When I returned to the station, the detective leaves the interview room with the boy and his mother and talks privately with me about the new information. It will be a strong tool in the interview. The detective, pretending to be friendly with the boy and his mother, asks me to get the boy a Coca Cola. I return with the drink and give it to the boy, leave the interview room and close the door behind me.

The evidence speaks for the girl as the 14-year-old boy speaks to the detective and confesses to penetrating the girl with his finger, but the evidence says that he has done more. Now he is going to be locked away in a juvenile detention center. He stands up and hugs his mother at the end of the interview. They both cry as the boy is taken away. At the same time, a young mother and father sit in a hospital room, crying after hearing the doctors' findings. The closest thing to justice I can find in this situation is that hopefully the girl is too young to remember what has happened to her, but even the thought of that is tragic.

I sit at the computer across from the interview room to begin my report. The door to the room is open. Everyone is gone. All that remains is the Coca Cola can sitting on a desk.

When I try to make sense of this case, the only explanation I can find is that perhaps the boy has been a silent victim of abuse himself, but maybe there is no sense to be made of it. Even the truth itself sometimes remains silent, keeping those who search for answers as voiceless as the victims, themselves.

FORTY-SIX

No Way Out

IT IS the quiet after the storm, a Sunday afternoon following the Friday night rape of a 2-year-old girl, and the Saturday night near-fatal stabbing of a man by his brother-in-law. My partner and I have worked 10 hours of overtime on the two cases combined. This is extreme since overtime is now a rarity during the budget crisis.

The town in which all hell has broken loose in the past two days now seems like a ghost town. Under a pale gray sky, a light snow blows like dust with dry leaves and debris in barren streets. March weather in Michigan is much like the contrasting mood of the city. One day is 40 degrees with sunshine and tulips breaking through the soil. The next day gets three inches of snow.

As I drive, my partner sits with his eyes closed and his head back, enjoying the peace and silence. When things are busy we usually talk and joke, but in these rare moments we let the silence rule.

I continue driving and observing our ghost city. When it dares to stand still, I can see the shell of the city it once was. The few auto factories that are left standing still blow smoke from high stacks. Just a few cars are parked in the lots of those factories, but no new jobs will come from them. In fact, I wonder who the people are that still have jobs there.

Nearly one of every two houses on many blocks in predominately black communities sits abandoned. They attest to a time when the city was bursting at the seams with people. Not many people are here now. The population and economic explosions happen in the suburbs today. Still, somebody must own these empty homes. Why don't they demolish them? Why doesn't the city demolish them? On one corner sits an abandoned commercial structure near abandoned homes. The roof is caving in on it. Somebody must own this building. Why can't it be destroyed?

Soon I see a black man and woman walking together. The man is carrying a television on his head. It is one of the oddities we see in poor communities. They both look like street people. The woman is missing her upper teeth. Though I don't find them necessarily suspicious, I would hate to drive past them and receive a radio call for a stolen television five minutes after they are out of sight. As I begin to slow the cruiser to see if I get a reaction from them, my partner raises his head and lets down his window. They stare at us as if we are crazy for noticing them. They are visibly annoyed, but not the least bit startled by us. We still think they are crazy, but that doesn't make what they are doing a crime.

After the staring contest is complete, the woman puts closure on the moment by telling us that the television belongs to her. The man is moving it to her mother's house for her. She doesn't owe us an explanation. It is her way of telling us that we had better things to do than to waste time watching this man carry the television. My partner puts his head back and closes his eyes again. As he puts his window up he states very quietly of the couple, "That's crazy."

I keep driving until we are dispatched to meet with plain clothes detectives who want our help searching a house for a homicide suspect, a black male, age 17. When we reach the house, I cover the side door as my partner and the detectives go to the front. Not far from me is a dilapidated garage with an old car surrounded by junk. I hear something moving inside. I draw my weapon as I wait for a signal from my partner telling me to come around front and inside the home. My attention is now split between the garage and the front of the house. Then I see the face of a pit bull in the garage. He stares at me and I stare back. The dog doesn't bark until I get the signal to enter the home with my partner and the detectives.

Once inside the home we search for the suspect but do not find him. The detectives and my partner talk to the grandmother and uncle of the suspect, and I focus my attention on two small children, a boy, 7, and a girl, 5. They show me a computer game on which they are practicing their spelling. Later the boy grabs two stuffed animals. They are dogs, one named Spike, and the other named Comet. Hugging Spike, he says, "I have to keep an eye on him. He likes to run in the street." Patting Comet on the head he says, "Now, Comet, he's a good dog. He never runs in the street." He went on to explain the relationship of his dogs. "Spike is the father; Comet is the son."

"If there is a father and a son, where is the mother?" I ask.

"She's dead. She was bad. I had to throw her away."

Before I leave the home, I speak briefly with the boy's father and find that the boy's mother is a drug addict and has never been involved with the children. I find amazing the young boy's ability to articulate his experience through those stuffed animals. In addition to this experience, he shares living space with a man wanted for murder. Some very intelligent human beings are born into terrible situations with no set formula to find a way out. Likewise, the young murder suspect eventually sees that he has no way out. Not long after we leave his home, he turns himself in at the police station.

FORTY-SEVEN

Frequent Flyer

EARLY EVENING traffic is at its heaviest when my partner and I receive a call for a woman driving the wrong way on a major one-way street. Because we are short-staffed, we respond from across town. By the time we safely weave our way to her using lights and sirens, she is stopped on the wrong side of the road, facing north in southbound traffic. As I exit the cruiser, the first thing I notice is the license plate on the front of her green station wagon that reads *JESUS*. It is only by the grace of God that she hasn't caused an accident.

I approach the woman and I see that she is breathing, but her eyes are glossy and staring into space. Dispatch stated that she was possibly Hispanic. Now I understand why. She is a light complexioned black woman. I notice a black substance around her mouth that looks like potting soil. An ambulance attendant jokes that maybe she has been eating dirt. While he is still laughing at his own joke, I look on the dashboard of her car and see a container of chocolate cookies.

We search her purse and find several empty pill containers. Cookies are not the only things she has eaten.

The ambulance crew transports the woman to the hospital for treatment. I impound the woman's car to ensure that her property will be safe. When I arrive at the hospital to check on the woman's condition for my report, I speak to a doctor who tells me that the woman has taken approximately four Vicodin and four Soma pills. The hospital staff is quite familiar with her – she is a paranoid schizophrenic who has made several failed attempts at suicide.

In our business, we refer to such mentally ill people who have constant contact with police, social workers or medical personnel, as "frequent fliers." On the surface, the term is a joke, but deep down it is an indictment of the system's inability to deal effectively with mentally ill people through law enforcement, social programs and medicine.

When I call the woman's home phone to notify family members of her status, I don't get an answer. However, I do hear an interesting message in her voice on her answering machine: *"I just want to share with you my soul says: Victory, victory, victory over defeat. Healing over sickness. Today over the past. Reality over insanity. Determination over complaints. Truth over lies. Justice over injustice. Smiles over frowns. Bravery over cowardice. Love over hate. Take notes 'cause ain't nothin' like the real thang. Everything I said is real. Have a blessed day."*

I call the number back so my partner can listen to it. He has been in the restroom while I speak to the doctor. After listening, he shakes his head, hangs up the phone at the nurses' station, looks at me and says, "frequent flier."

FORTY-EIGHT

Guns and Power

A 4-YEAR-OLD black boy makes the news when an unloaded .25 caliber gun falls from his pocket on a school bus. The boy apparently found the gun in his grandfather's closet and decided to carry it to school. Out of naiveté, society is quick to question how a 4-year-old knows what a gun is and what he plans to do with it. Perhaps it is his dream to be able to possess a gun. The gun represents power, but power against what?

In our adult years, we can underestimate the curiosity and knowledge of small children. I can recall once in 1972, at age 7, I found a handgun under my parents' mattress. I was home alone. Just how I thought to look there is beyond me. Nevertheless, I found a gun. I touched that gun and felt the heaviness and power of it. I put it back beneath the mattress. I lived in a home where my father was very violent to my mother. I vowed to return to the mattress the next time I saw my father hurt my mother. However, when the moment came, I went back to get the gun and it was gone. I never saw it again, but I often wonder how my life might have been changed if I had been able to find that gun that day.

Today, I can legally carry a gun 24 hours a day. I understand the psychological power of a gun. Though the gun becomes something of a burden, I feel naked and vulnerable without it, and fear being caught in a situation where I might need it and not have it. The biggest fear of an unarmed person who knows the power of the gun is to cross paths with a person who has that power. I feel more powerful with a gun if I am taking a long walk in the dark or daylight, in my own community, or driving across the state with my family to unfamiliar communities.

The psychological power of the gun is so strong that I can hardly remember what life was like before I could legally carry one. During the eight-month period when I was laid off work, my biggest adjustment was learning to live without the gun on my right hip. I have never used my gun against a human being and hope I never will, but still there is a certain power in knowing that I could, as many officers may say, "cancel a person's birth date," if the need arises. A part of me understands why black boys and men seek the power of the gun. For many legitimate reasons, they feel powerless in society.

With the thought of the 4-year-old in mind, my partner and I are dispatched to a housing complex for an 11-year-old black boy with a BB gun. A maintenance man sees him shooting out windows and detains him until we arrive. The boy sits quietly in the rental office with his mother. The BB gun he carried looks like a 9mm. It looks similar to a .45 caliber look-alike B.B. gun I had as a 12-year-old in 1977. That same year, when three boys chased me home, I ran inside and grabbed that BB gun and ran outside with it. The three boys ran from me. They were so afraid of me that they reported me to the school police officer who gave me a good talking to. The boys all apologized and I never had another problem with them or anyone else. That was the power of the gun. It was an equalizer for a powerless kid left to fend for himself with only a working mother for moral support.

The mother of the 11-year-old boy states that she cannot work because her son has been labeled "special education," and he will not attend the special classes without her.

Black boys growing up poor without positive male influence who wear the negative labels of society will become candidates for the power of guns.

Later in the shift we are dispatched to a school parking lot for an argument. Before we pull into the lot, a woman driving away from the school flags us down and states that some men, who had been arguing over a basketball game inside the gym, were about to fight and possibly start shooting. Just as we pull into the lot, several shots ring out. The lot is filled with cars, so it is impossible to tell where the shots are coming from. People start to run and drive frantically from the lot in all directions as I call for backup. Later we find that a man has been hit in the hand by a stray bullet. I collect 13 9mm shells and one shotgun shell and turn them in as evidence.

On our last call of the night, we respond to a suicidal black male who dispatch tells us is 22 years old and just five feet, two inches tall. Dispatch states that he is standing in the street firing a handgun into the air. While en route, I joke with my partner that maybe the man is mad because he is so short. I have seen enough guns for one day and I am distressed about yet another call involving a gun. I have worked eight straight days and my patience has worn thin. I have the next four days off and I just want to get off work without an incident. I say aloud that I hope that if the man is going to kill himself he will decide to do it without our help. My partner laughs.

Dispatch states that a single gunshot had been heard followed by screams. When we arrive, the man has gone inside his home. The man's girlfriend opens the door and says that the man never had a gun and that they had only argued. As we search the house, I see the man walking from a bedroom into the kitchen. I still do not trust that he doesn't have a gun. He tries to run out the side door. I grab him, handcuff and search him. I never find a gun but the man has three warrants, none for which I can lodge him in jail because of the budget crisis.

When I check with the neighbors who reported the gunfire, they will not admit to me in person that they saw the man with a gun. If they would, I could arrest him. The neighbors don't want any trouble. They just ask the police to investigate and send a message. Also, the man's girlfriend refuses to file a complaint against him. Without anything more to go on, we are forced to release the man knowing possibly that he has committed a crime. Several cruisers line the street. The message has been sent.

On the first night I am off work, I dream that I am in a shoot-out in which I narrowly miss shooting a fellow police officer by mistake. For me, the dream is just more proof of the psychological power of guns.

FORTY-NINE

Signs

MY PARTNER has the day off. I am working alone and not too thrilled about it. My first call is for a missing 83-year-old black man. I drive slowly and try to imagine under what circumstances this man might be missing. I also wonder what the emotional state of his family might be. Just as I park my cruiser, a drizzle of rain dramatically turns into an all-out thunderstorm. It's like a movie script; I exit my cruiser and walk slowly in the rain, any optimism about this case being dampened by the sudden storm.

I approach the door and am greeted by the missing man's wife, a pleasant 77-year-old black woman. I immediately think of my own grandmother. The woman speaks in a very calm, dignified manner as she explains that her husband left at about 9 a.m. to walk to the bank, which is about two miles away. It is now about 5 p.m., and he has not been heard from. As the woman speaks, her hands catch my attention. They are gentle and arthritic and she wrings them repeatedly as she tells the story.

Inside, I find other concerned people who have gathered to wait with the woman.

She says the walk is common practice for him, and he is in good mental and physical health. To me, this only makes the situation seem more suspicious.

I try not to further excite the woman, but all signs point to the possibility of foul play. Maybe he has been robbed, abducted, or murdered? Though police officers are supposed to keep an open mind during investigations, the constant exposure to human tragedy can condition one to think the worst. Foul play is my first thought. The fact that our city has had several recent murder cases involving elderly victims doesn't brighten my perspective. The area is highly populated with what are considered undesirable people who might see an elderly man cashing a check as an easy target.

I notify a supervisor of the circumstances surrounding the case and continue taking the report. She tells me there are no friends or family he might visit in the area of the bank. She is absolutely certain there is no safe place that he could be. Still, in a very gentle manner, she clears off a space on the coffee table for me to write, and offers me a seat on the couch. In the police academy, I was trained never to take a seat in a person's house. The reasons are obvious. An officer who sits in an unfamiliar environment is more vulnerable than one standing. However, in this case, to remain standing might insult the woman and would not help my investigation, I do not hesitate to take the seat. The woman sits next to me. The other people in the room listen as I take information from the woman.

As I complete my report, I ask the woman for her date of birth. She tells me June 30, 1925. It is a coincidence that my birth date is June 30, 1965. I hesitate before telling the woman, as I don't want her to perceive it as a shallow attempt to ease the tension. Then I do tell her. She looks at me and says, "Honey, maybe it's a sign." At that moment, we hear the back door slam. She jumps from the couch and runs through the kitchen and I follow.

It is her husband. He has safely returned home, though he is soaking wet from being caught in the storm. He explains that he had tripped and fallen while walking and became disoriented.

His wife begins to cry and holds her hands over her mouth. She grabs him and hugs him tightly. "Don't you ever do this to me again," she says to her husband who doesn't seem to understand what all the fuss is about. Others in the home begin jumping and shouting for joy and praising God. We all talk about the birth date and how it had to be a sign from God that everything would be fine. The other people keep thanking me, though I know I can't take credit. Until the man returned home, I felt little faith in the possibility of a good ending to this case.

After a few moments, it is time to say goodbye to this family and wish them well, though I would like to stay a while.

I step outside the house, out of their sight, and am so moved by what I have just seen that I start to cry. I can still hear the celebration inside as I walk off the porch. Before I can leave the yard, someone from inside runs out of the house and thanks me again. By this time, the storm has ceased just as dramatically as it had begun. The sun is now shining brightly through diminished drizzle.

I get into my cruiser and drive for about five minutes before I can stop crying.

I realize that I have learned to rely too much on my human experience, and I have forgotten that God is present, even in what may seem to be a hopeless situation. I am thankful that when my human logic fails, God allows the sun to shine on the darkness of the negative experiences that sometimes cloud my mind.

FIFTY

High Noon

A MAN is reported lying in the middle of a busy street. When we arrive, we find a black man lying in the fetal position. Luckily, a vehicle has not struck him. We pull him up from the ground and try to talk to him and decide he is mentally ill. He does not respond to us in English. Instead, he speaks in gibberish. The man may believe he is speaking another language. When we get him to the hospital, he speaks to the staff in this gibberish. After filling out a petition for a mental evaluation, we leave him in the hands of medical professionals.

Late in the evening, we receive a call for a strange man who has knocked on someone's door claiming that he had been shot several times. When we arrive, we find a young black man, late 20s, who is mentally ill. It takes four officers to wrestle him to the ground and handcuff him. He is a well-known "frequent flyer" who has recently taken an officer's gun on a call. The officer and his partner were able to get the gun back without incident.

In another incident, a uniformed police officer was stabbed three times by a mentally ill man before he was able to stop the man by shooting him once in the stomach.

In still another incident, three officers were placed on administrative leave and investigated after a mentally ill man they were forced to restrain died in their custody.

This weighs on my mind as we wrestle with this man. Officers have committed this man to the mental ward several times already, but it hasn't seemed to help him. He is a fixture on the streets.

"I know you. You've been having sex with my sister. I've seen your picture on her walls," he shouts to nobody in particular.

"You have a baby by my girlfriend!" he screams.

Once we get him inside the cruiser, he tries to kick the windows out. We rush him to the hospital where he is stripped of his clothing and placed in four-point restraints.

"Look at this shit. Look how they shot me up. Look at all these bullet holes in my body," he says, looking at his own naked chest.

The man isn't injured. As we leave him, I am awed by the power of the human mind and how it is often best seen through the mentally ill rather than the so-called sane people of the world.

Then, my partner and I are dispatched to meet a woman who is having trouble with her adult son. He has become angry and smashed a window out of the home. When we arrive, we find that the man has locked his mother out of the house. The mother is frail. Her eyes are filled with tears. She says that her son is mentally ill and hasn't been taking his medication.

Finally, another family member lets us in the house. We go in with our guns drawn. The woman says that her son is known to carry a gun. We search the house and find him hiding in a basement closet. He is a small man, sitting like a small child on the floor of the closet with his knees folded to his chest. His chin rests atop his knees and his fingers are interlocked at the front of his legs.

We pull him from the closet and handcuff him.

"Why are y'all arresting me? What did I do?" he says in a calm manner.

"You're not under arrest. We just want to take you to get some help."

"Mama, you gonna let them take me? Please don't let them take me, Mama," he shouts, now crying and hysterical.

"I hate the hospital. I hate medicine. It makes me burn inside."

I take the man outside and place him in an ambulance. As I ride with him to the hospital, he begins talking to himself in a very soft voice.

"Yeah, I was in that closet. So what?"

As we get closer to the hospital: "Don't take me to this place. I'll start taking my meds. I promise."

Once we get the man inside the hospital, I find a social worker to help the mother complete a petition to have her son admitted to the mental ward.

Committing a family member to the mental ward is a difficult and painful decision. The mother cries from a broken heart on her way out the door, and her adult son cries like a small child and screams, "Mama, don't leave me here with these people!"

In another similar incident, my partner and I are dispatched to a home for domestic violence. A 30-year-old black man is threatening his mother. When we arrive, we find that the man has a severe mental illness. He is standing in the middle of a busy intersection making sexual gestures. He begins to run.

I am driving. My partner chases him on foot. I box him in with the cruiser. We handcuff and transport him to a local hospital where his family files a petition to have him committed to a mental institution. The mother says the man began having mental problems when he was just 14 years old. More recently, he has had several nervous breakdowns.

One evening, my partner and I are dispatched to assist an officer who is working alone and having trouble with a man. When we arrive, we find a black man sitting on a park bench near a lake. It looks as if he lives there. He has several items of clothing spread across the bench. Debris surrounds the bench on the ground. A coat hangs on a tree not far from him. He is homeless and mentally ill. His bark is worse than his bite. He initially curses us and tells us to stay away from him, but as we handcuff him, he makes no protest. We place him in the cruiser and gather his belongings from the area.

As we drive him to the hospital, he talks to himself:

"It was midnight blue with flowers on the front and bunnies on the back. It was pretty. I know you like that. I fill it up with three gallons of gasoline and the rest water. High octane. It's high noon. A man draws a gun on me and I draw one on him. The Sundance Kid. They call me the Sundance Kid."

FIFTY-ONE

Answering Our Brother's Call

I AM sure I hear the dispatcher say the word, "Suicide!" I drive alone in the dark to the address, and hope one of us is mistaken. The large square house sits on a hill with a long driveway leading to the back where I see lights. Just as I park on the street in front of the house, the dispatcher clears up the matter: "Suicide. Confirmed suicide."

I have seen people die in a variety of ways, but this is my first suicide. As I force my feet to walk toward the back door, my body wants to turn and go in the opposite direction. The feelings of fear and uncertainty swirl inside me. Where will the victim be? What method did the victim choose? Not knowing what to prepare for adds to my unease. No matter how many dead people I see, I never become accustomed to it. It is impossible to have such intimate contact with death and not think of my own mortality or the mortality of people closest to me.

Finally, I reach the door and see a light on in the kitchen. The house is quiet. I walk inside and find a man sitting alone at the kitchen table. He is crying and intoxicated. I am still trying to get a glimpse of a suicide victim, but I don't see one.

"My brother. He killed himself," says the man, his voice small like that of a child who has been scolded.

"Where is he?" I ask.

"In the basement."

"Which way is the basement?"

The man, still acting like a child, points toward the back door, refusing to look in that direction.

"Can you show me where he is?" I ask the man in a soft encouraging voice, but he refuses. At that point, I realize his fear is much larger than mine is. An event that is merely a part of my job is a part of this man's life. I use that thought to push myself to do what I know I must do next—view the body.

I walk back toward the back door and turn right and take nine stairs down, counting each one. The basement is cold and unfinished and lit by a bare light bulb with a long string attached. The cement walls are bare and thin spider webs hang from most places. I can both feel and smell the dampness of the basement. Immediately to my right, I see the man's body hanging by the neck. To end his life, he used a tie-down strap with a metal ratchet-end looped over exposed ceiling pipes.

His head leans to one side. His eyes are open. I look him in the eyes and wonder what type of pain caused him to go to this extreme. He appears to be in his late 20s or early 30s. Rigor mortis has set in. His arms hang at his sides, his fingers fixed in various directions. His legs are bent slightly. He looks like a mannequin. Behind him is a table and chair. Several beer bottles and cigarette butts are on the table and on the floor near the table. Perhaps this is how he spent his last moments, thinking about his problems and making his fatal decision. The words of the dispatcher play again in my head: "Suicide. Confirmed suicide."

I go back upstairs to get the story from his grieving brother. He tells me his brother was having marital problems. He was separated from his wife. They have a young child. To top it all off, he had just lost his job. He came to live with his brother like he had on other occasions when life's problems got the best of him. He drank beer, played pool in the dining room, and complained about his problems like he always did.

However, something changed this time. The grieving brother said he grew tired of his brother's complaining. He had his own problems. He could no longer carry his brother's mental baggage.

They argued briefly and the grieving brother decided enough was enough. He walked out the door while his brother begged him to listen. He got in his car and drove off, leaving the distraught brother behind. Moments later the grieving brother's cell phone began to ring. He picked it up and saw that it is was his brother calling. He refused to answer. A few hours later, with hopes that things had time to cool off, he returned to find the house quiet. Though he thought his brother could be sleeping, he found the silence suspicious. He checked the upstairs bedrooms. Then he ran to the basement yelling his brother's name and found him hanging.

By now a couple of detectives have arrived and are playing pool on the very pool table where the dead man played his last game. It is the typical cold police response to tragedy. They have no sympathy for the dead man. Instead, they sympathize with those left behind to deal with his death.

"What about his wife?" one says. "What about his child? His child has to live with fact that his old man killed himself. What about his brother who is traumatized by finding him like that? Man, what about his parents? They have to get this terrible phone call in the middle of the night. Fuck this guy. I have no sympathy for him. He took the easy way out. Three ball in the side pocket."

Another detective says, "He did a damn good job." However, it is the words of the grieving brother that haunt me most. They are a metaphor for all humanity. "I should have answered my brother's call," he said. "I should have answered my brother's call. I should have answered my brother's call."

FIFTY-TWO

Her Wits End

I ANSWER a call from dispatch about some neighbors concerned over a teenage boy. I find the 14-year-old standing outside his home. I can see lights on in the house. People are moving around inside. He says he has rung the doorbell and knocked at the door, but no one answers. It is nearly 11 p.m. He says he has been on the street for several days now. His mother won't let him come inside. I sit in front of the home and use my cell phone to call inside, but still there is no answer.

He tells me his mother is a medical professional and she is at work. I call the mother at work.

"Hi, ma'am. This is Officer Willingham with the Flint Police Department. Do you know where your son is?"

"Not at my house. I don't know where he is."

"Well, he's your child. You are responsible for him. You are supposed to know where he is."

"Well, I don't want him at my house."

"You don't have a choice ma'am. The law says you have to let him in the house."

"Well I'm not letting him in my house."

"You mean to tell me you are a medical professional, you are in the business of saving lives, it's after 11 p.m., and you are going to leave your own child on the streets. How would you feel if you saw your own child come into the emergency room dead or seriously injured?"

"It would be his fault."

"No, it would be your fault."

"Well I'm at work. What do you want me to do?"

"You can either call your home and tell your other children to let him in the house or I can report you to Children's Protective Services."

"Well, I'll see if I can leave my job. I want to turn him over to the state anyway."

"Well if you want to turn him over to the state, there's a proper way to do that. You're a professional. You should know that. The way that you're dealing with it now is wrong. In fact you're not dealing with it at all."

"What do you want me to do? I'm at work."

"Either you make a call and let him in the house or you leave work now and I'll have protective services meet us so that you can turn your child over to the state."

Apparently, the boy has had some trouble in school. He has had some problems following house rules, but this is no reason to leave him on the streets. In fact, it is illegal to leave the boy on the street.

The mother does return home. I take her and her child to a local hospital to meet with Children's Protective Services. A social worker informs her that the consequences for turning her child over to the state will be that she will face neglect charges. Additionally, she has three other children and one grandchild who would be taken from the home. In the face of these odds, the mother decides to take the son home. She has a multitude of problems with all of her children. This incident just seems to be the thing that drives her over the edge. Never have I seen a mother take this approach. Until now, I took it for granted that mothers have an unlimited capacity for stress. Clearly, this mother has reached a limit.

The social worker can only sum up it by saying, "I guess she was at her wits end."

FIFTY-THREE

Driving While Black

It is a weekday morning. I am driving my wife to work. Like many average Americans, we enjoy coffee and a popular radio morning show. We have left in plenty of time. Our mood is relaxed. We talk about the kids, work, people at work, and so forth. At the hospital where she works, I kiss her good-bye and start back home, just as I do every weekday morning.

It's a day off for me. I exhale and continue drinking my coffee. It is a beautiful day. I think of a million things I can do. However, before I can settle on anything, my peace is broken by the sound of a siren in the distance. It is difficult to tell from what direction it is coming. Then I see the police cruiser in my rearview mirror. I realize now why people don't always immediately pull over or stop.

I pull to the right side of the road as the cruiser gets closer. I wonder where it is going. I wait for them to pass, but they stop behind me. I think maybe this is a joke as two white male officers tactically approach both sides of my mini-van. Immediately, I recognize the officers. I partnered with one of them for an entire summer. Now, however, the serious look on their faces is foreign to me. This causes my heart to race. I am a black man, wearing old sweats and a baseball cap, and I have a loaded 9mm gun in my vehicle.

I've heard many black citizens talk about *driving while black*. I've also heard the horror stories about black officers being mistaken for criminals and being killed while off duty. Until now, I never thought much about either thing. I am hoping against hope that this is a joke.

"Drivers license, proof of insurance and registration," the officer on the driver's side says to me. At the same time, I notice that the second officer is glancing at three bicycles that belong to my three children piled in the back of my van. The looks on their faces intensify. My heart is still racing and I accept the fact that this is no joke, though part of me still hopes they might simultaneously yell, "Gotcha," at which time we would all be able to have a good laugh.

I show the officers my badge and police identification. Their faces turn red. In the awkwardness of the moment, the officer on the driver's side stutters slightly before saying, "Hey man, we're not used to seeing you without your glasses on." The other follows his lead and blurts out, "Yeah, we're used to seeing you in your other car." I don't bother to ask the reason for the stop nor do they bother to try to explain. I only own one vehicle and I have never worn glasses. Had I not been in possession of my badge, I wonder how far the incident might have gone. I also wondered how many times they have done this before. We end the encounter without closure.

They walk away, and I drive away still not wanting to believe what has just happened. Had members of my own department just profiled me? For a moment my denial allows me to question myself: Maybe I did something wrong? However, I knew I hadn't done anything wrong. I was making the same trek I've made hundreds of times. The area is familiar; I was relaxed.

I feel violated and humiliated. I am ashamed to keep the secret and afraid to report it. How much weight would one black police officer's word hold against two white ones? In the end, I decide that, if I report the incident, the public pain that it might cause would certainly be greater than the private one I choose to bear. Either way, the reality of *driving while black* hurts me deeply.

FIFTY-FOUR

The Ebb and Flow

I HAVE learned to feel and embrace the unpredictable ebb and flow of police work. As a result of analyzing my own experiences, I have become a better investigator. My decision-making abilities have improved. I am more eager to hear the stories of people, make good arrests, and collect supporting evidence of crimes both large and small.

In short, I am discovering my purpose in policing and enjoying my job more now than at any other time in my career. I find this task so important that I have decided to pass on taking a promotion exam because it would require that I buy many books and spend a great amount of time studying them, thus less time for my writing project. When I am able to publish my book, I will consider it a promotion. Many officers spend their careers in search of promotions and assignments to specialized bureaus, though it has been said that the most important job in any police department is that of the patrol officer. As an ex-Army sergeant, I believe that just as the infantry is thought to be the backbone of the Army, so is the patrol officer the backbone of policing.

In the first year or two of my career, every call was significant to me. When asked to speak at a church once, I told the congregation that I literally saw something to pray about every day. I never saw how that could change, but it did. The adjustment from civilian life to policing is a process of learning to swallow emotion. What every new police officer experiences is not within normal realms, regardless of his or her previous life experience.

I remember cringing at the thought of responding to calls involving serious injury or death. Before I learned to swallow the emotion attached to human suffering, I thought once about quitting. I didn't think I would be able to survive the job. Once I learned to manage my emotions and began to adjust, individual days lost their significance and the abnormal became normal. They began to meld into nondescript weeks, months and years of "stuff" a civilian can't possibly understand. My career reached a point where every day became merely next in succession.

I estimate that during my six-year career I have answered more than 14,000 radio calls. Each call involves interaction with people, sometimes multiple people with multiple stories. I have developed an ear for truth and lies and the nonverbal cues that support them. The scenarios begin to repeat themselves. They become mundane. Soon I forget what I feel or that I am able to feel. With the exception of the highly unusual, the everyday experience is lost in a pile of thousands. Writing has helped me to rediscover the details of the everyday experience. The daily examination of them gives me the opportunity to explore feelings and thoughts I had learned to pass over in preparation for the next day's work.

I am often surprised at what I find hidden inside myself when I take the time to examine each day. I find at least one incident in a day that impacts me. Then, there are days when I am overwhelmed with impact-filled experiences. Such is the ebb and flow of police work; things either happen incredibly fast, or unbelievably slow.

The day before was one such day.

It begins with a call from dispatch for a car to respond to a stabbing. I am behind the station inspecting my cruiser. I have only a quarter tank of gas because I haven't had time to fuel up. I stop the inspection and fly across town, lights and siren. I arrive and find a crowd of angry family members standing in the front yard. A black male, 20, has been stabbed in the right side of his head by his girlfriend's 13-year-old brother. Other officers protect the scene as I attempt to catch the ambulance that transported the victim before I arrived. I find the ambulance just a few blocks from the hospital. I need to get the victim's story and medical condition. I also need to collect the names of the ambulance crew for my report.

I find that the victim is not seriously injured. The crew wheels him into triage rather than trauma. He doesn't want to press charges against the boy who is under arrest and being transported to the station by other officers. I alert a sergeant who releases the child.

As I leave the hospital to return to the station for fuel, dispatch again calls for a car to respond to another stabbing. We are short-staffed and all cars are currently tied up on calls. I answer the call, but I am working alone, which will limit my activity since the suspect is still on the scene. Dispatch orders a two-person car to leave a less important call to help with the stabbing. Before I can arrive, I am canceled.

I make it back to the gas-pump, but as I am fueling up, I am dispatched to help paramedics at a home. I feel a flush of emotion go over my body. The address of the house tells me it is directly across the street from a house my family once owned when I was a child. I am told the firefighters can see a motionless elderly man lying on the floor. Unsure whether or not it is a crime scene, they are hesitant to enter.

I wonder what has happened to the man. I ask dispatch to send another car in the event there is a crime scene or a suspect lurking. While en route, I imagine what the man must look like. I imagine what the inside of the house must look like. I recall what the inside of my old house once looked like. I can remember every room. I can remember playing in the yard and walking to elementary school. Before I can arrive, I am canceled again. All that emotional buildup for nothing.

Four minutes later, I am dispatched to take a report for a missing 7-year-old black boy. The pace of my day suddenly changes. A missing child is a different ball of wax compared to the rushing around that I have already done. It requires a tedious initial investigation. I must ask many questions, the answers to which are usually filtered through an emotional mother and other concerned family members. While en route I imagine what the child must look like and where he might be. Many times missing children are found at a friend's or family member's home. Sometimes children even return home before the police arrive. Yet sometimes children are abducted and killed.

When I arrive at the house, I sense a certain coldness and neglect. The house is in disrepair. Gray duct tape covers the bottom portion of a broken screen door that swings slightly back and forth as I walk to the porch. No one comes out to meet me. There is no sense of urgency, and that adds to the coldness. I begin to think that maybe there is no missing child, or maybe he has returned.

I knock at the door and the mother answers. She tells me her son is missing, but she isn't particularly emotional about it. She says he was last seen about one hour ago playing in the backyard. I ask her to walk there with me and show me the exact spot where she last saw him. It is early spring. The ground is very soggy. I see his footprints along the fence line. A large wooded park that has long since lost its innocence with the findings of dead bodies over the years borders the yard.

I check in and around a garage that is leaning to one side. Another officer reminds me to check the inside of the home. Sometimes missing children are merely hiding beneath beds and in closets. I have learned that the child has special needs and is on medication for seizures. His mother says he has a habit of wandering off, and I don't understand why she hasn't kept a closer eye on him. She states that she was preparing to get in the bathtub when she noticed him missing. I make a quick canvass of the streets immediately adjacent to his and don't find him. I notify a sergeant and request a dog to track his scent from the backyard. Maybe we have a chance of finding him before something happens.

The dog zigzags through the backyard before heading south to a busy intersection then back north through the dangerous park. It isn't a good sign. While the dog is busy, I talk with neighbors to get a feel for the character of the child and the family.

One neighbor explains her observation of his mental slowness. Several times she's had to chase the boy away from her yard. He likes to play with her dog. He doesn't realize that the dog is a danger to him. She says the boy's mother does not do a good job of watching him. On occasion, she has seen the boy pull down his pants and take a bowel movement on the sidewalk. She thinks the boy would be easy prey for a sexual predator, seeing that he so easily pulls down his pants.

However, the most important thing she tells me is that the mother had another mentally slow child that wandered off at age 5, and was later found dead.

The mother never mentioned this to me. She doesn't act like a woman who has lost a child. Even when I ask her how many children she has, she never mentioned the dead child. I find it odd and don't know at this point whether it is significant or not.

After nearly an hour-long search, the dog loses the scent and there is nothing more I can do. Finally I see tears from the mother, but she is not otherwise visibly distressed. I take the report and clear the scene. I wonder where this boy can be. I wonder if his mother really wants him, or if in some odd way she hopes something will happen to him. Three hours later I am informed that the boy has returned home. Under the circumstances, I wonder how long he will be there.

On my final call of the night, I am dispatched to assist out-county police officers who have a search warrant to dig in the backyard of a home in a poor, predominately black section of town. As I arrive with another officer, I see that a crowd has already begun to gather. People are asking questions. A couple of abandoned, burned-out homes sit across the street from the home to be searched. From a few streets over I can hear loud rap music and the sound of squealing tires coming from several vehicles. Moments later, I hear a couple gunshots. It is all par for the course in this community.

In this environment, it is awkward for five white male suburban officers in plain clothes, flashing credentials, and arriving in unmarked vehicles, to knock at the door of a black family in the heart of the ghetto. The other officer and I are here because they need local uniforms to stand by.

The officers have just arrested a man for a 1987 murder in which a woman's purse was taken. An informant has told them that the purse is buried in this backyard. The suspect's parents still live in the home. They are of course baffled as to why five white men need to dig up their yard, but they are cooperative.

The officers bring in their equipment and began digging and sifting through the soil. The informant, a person who was once close to the arrested man, stands in the crowd and inconspicuously guides the officers to several spots with non-verbal cues.

After several hours of digging and sifting well into the darkness with large generator powered lights, they call off the search. They are able to find only a few particles, but can't be sure they are related to the case. We joke about how on television, the police would find the purse totally intact, with the victim's identification inside, and suspect's fingerprints all over it. In real life it doesn't work like that.

One detective tells me the arrested man is also suspected in the murder of a black male cab driver between 1989 and 1990. This strikes a cord with me because a first cousin's husband owned a cab company and was brutally murdered while driving his cab in 1991. The last I heard, his murder had gone unsolved. When he was killed, his daughter was just 4 years old, and his son was only 9 months old. I give the detective the information and he promises to work on it. I am nervous about talking to my cousin about this. She has moved forward beautifully in her life, becoming a certified pharmacy technician. Her daughter is preparing to graduate high school. Both her children are well adjusted and academically gifted. It would mean a lot to me to see the murder solved, but what would it mean for her and her children? Furthermore, what would it mean if I stir up old feelings only to have the murder not be solved? The thought of it is cruel, or maybe I am being negative.

When I contact my cousin, I am embarrassed to find that her husband's murder has already been solved. Sadly, the suspects had already been released. She explains that she lives in daily fear that the suspects might harm her or her children. She has saved all the press clippings from the murder. She plans to share them with her children when the time is right. I wonder if the time will ever be right.

FIFTY-FIVE

The Seasons Change

THE FIRST warm day of spring arrives. The temperature has jumped from near freezing to 65 degrees. The change in seasons seems to have a great impact on young people. After a long winter of confinement, warm spring days liberate them. Sadly, this liberation isn't often positive.

Young black people in groups of 20 or more stand on corners and loiter in known drug areas. Come to think of it, there are very few places they can stand in their community that isn't considered a drug area. Therefore, the kids will be viewed as a danger to society almost anywhere they gather. The danger, however, should not be attributed to their skin color, but rather to the fact that they are surrounded by vice. Children of any color raised in the same degrading environment can become equally dangerous to society.

Except for portable basketball hoops that line many streets, they have no safe havens. The hoops are another great source of neighborhood complaints. When residents call, we are forced to break up basketball games that are most times peaceful but out of place in residential areas. I attribute the phenomenon to children attempting to create that safe haven.

Public parks are filled with trash, tall weeds and drug activity. Though some still play basketball there, they are not safe. My partner and I back up officers at one park who have caught a young black man selling "crack." The man places the drugs in his mouth and they dissolve, causing his tongue to become numb. The officers call an ambulance for him.

We respond to several calls for a large group of fighting kids, but when we arrive we find no fight. The people who call know we will respond faster if they say a large group is fighting.

The change in weather also impacts the mindset of police officers. The first warm day of the year makes many officers openly speculate that it will be a "wild" summer. As my partner and I continue patrolling, he says, "Somebody's going to get shot today. I can feel it. An officer is going to get shot or shot at."

"Well, it won't be us," I respond. "If we are involved in a shooting, it will be because we are doing the shooting, not because we are being shot at."

A lot of police work is instinct and feeling. I don't disregard my partner's statement, but I hope he is not right.

Just after that we make a traffic stop on a vehicle with no plate. The windshield is cracked and the hood of the car is partially up. Also the trunk lock has been punched out. I don't make traffic stops much because they are proven to be the most dangerous activity an officer can undertake. In this case the car appears to be stolen. As we approach the car on foot, I am thinking about my partner's earlier statement. I hope this is not the moment he is talking about.

Three young black males are inside the vehicle. The driver has a suspended license, is on probation, and has five arrest warrants.

We are on a side street close to a busy intersection in the black community. People gather as we place the man in the back seat of our cruiser. On the first warm day of the year a traffic stop is a source of entertainment for people who don't have anything else to do. A man and woman in the crowd clown around as if they are assaulting each other. People laugh as they put on a show for us. We write the driver of the car two tickets, release him and impound the vehicle. Once again, budget cuts prevent us from lodging him in jail.

As we drive away, the crowd facetiously cheers and claps for what they perceive to be a mere performance by us. In return, we thank them for their performance. The show is over, but it is nice that we could entertain each other. As this night progresses, my partner and I answer 11 radio calls, 10 of which are for fights. I am thankful that my partner's words haven't come true. I think it is just the weather.

FIFTY-SIX

Sometimes it Snows in April

I GO to the locker room to look for my partner. He missed roll call. I think maybe he is running late, but just then I learn from a sergeant that he's not coming in today. I accidentally drop a can of mace and it rolls beneath a toilet stall door. As I go inside the stall to retrieve the can, I notice graffiti above a box of toilet seat liners: *The only protection the department gives you. Better than the health plan.* On another wall: *How 'bout 10 hour shifts. How about the pay raise. Most can't work 4 hours. Can't expect them to work 10.*

As a part of the budget cuts, benefit packages for officers have been reduced. Officers in our department have unsuccessfully lobbied for 10-hour shifts four days a week. Four-day workweeks would give officers more time off. They would be less stressful than the seven- and eight-day stretches we currently work. In addition, our contract expired more than five years ago. Because of the city's financial crisis, an arbitrator sided with the city. We are stuck working with an expired contract and no raises. Law prevents police officers from striking.

There is nothing more we do about it. In short, morale is down.

I agree with the writing on the wall, and I am even further stressed by the fact that my partner has failed to show and hasn't personally called me. It is a cardinal sin in our profession. As a courtesy, we are always expected to give our partners a *heads-up* if we're not coming to work, especially on a Saturday night when the most dangerous activity is expected to happen. I am unhappy to find at the last minute that I will be working alone when, mentally, I have found comfort in the thought that I will have a partner to depend on. When I expect to work alone, I have time to mentally adjust. It is difficult to make the mental adjustment from partner to no partner at the last minute. This is just another part of the psychology of policing.

I start my shift in a funk. My wife and kids are out of town. I woke up to an empty house and ate breakfast and lunch alone. Now that my partner has bailed out on me, I feel alone on all sides. I thought I would enjoy the space, but I don't. In my entire career I have never taken to the streets without physically seeing my family, saying good-bye to them and knowing that they are safe at home. I work second shift, which means I am rarely ever home in the evening. Most mornings my nine-year-old daughter asks me if I caught any bad guys the night before. A "yes" answer of course requires more explanation. In the end, she always wants to know why the bad people do whatever they do. There, my explanations fall short. I'm just happy that she cares.

My first call on this day is on a missing persons report. It is a classic call for an officer working alone. Officers who work alone are generally dispatched to take reports for crimes not in progress, which usually means lots of paperwork by the end of the shift. I have my partner to thank for this.

I arrive and find a black woman barbecuing on a small front porch. The pit has no legs and sits directly on the porch. She tells me her adult brother is mentally disabled and has been missing for more than an hour. Another of her brothers has legal guardianship over the missing man. I sit in my cruiser and wait for the guardian to arrive. I am still in a mental fog, disappointed that I am even on this call. I watch two black children just up the street play a game called curb-ball. I remember playing curb-ball. Two children stand across the street from each other just beyond the curb. They throw a basketball back and forth and try to score points by striking the curb in front of their opponent. I think curb-ball must be unique to African-Americans because I have worked in every sector of this city and have never seen anyone else play the game. Before long, the missing man returns safely carrying a radio to his ear, looking as if he doesn't have a care in the world.

As I pull away, I drive past the kids playing curb-ball and stop to speak with a group of black men. We debate for a moment about who will win the Final Four. Sometimes it is good to engage people on a human level when I'm not enforcing the law. The times are rare when police officers have an opportunity to just talk to people. Before I can finish the conversation, I am dispatched with other cars to a large fight. There is rarely ever an actual fight—just a large group of black teens gathered in the street near a portable basketball hoop. We break up the group to make the residents feel better. However, I wonder, where will the kids go? The next call is for the same situation in a totally different neighborhood. We make them move the hoop from the street, but again I ask the question: "Where will the kids go?"

Later I am dispatched to check a possible stolen car. I arrive to find a car with no doors, no seats or engine sitting on the street in front of an abandoned house. Again, this is a typical call for an officer working alone. I complete the paperwork and impound the car. I am still a little depressed about how my day has started, when I am sent to my old neighborhood to meet with a man who says someone pulled a gun on him. I find that the man is an old childhood friend. He is a tall, slender, very light complexioned black man with strong Native American features. He wears his hair in braids with a black headband. In all these years, he has never left the neighborhood. We talk about old times. He seems upset but doesn't talk to me about the incident, maybe because he knows me. I don't press him. We end the conversation and he walks off. He always walks. He has never learned to drive a car.

Next, I am dispatched to talk with a family about a violent teen. He has smashed the window out of his grandfather's car. When I arrive, I find that I am familiar with the family. It is the teen's younger brother who shot a window at an apartment complex with a BB gun earlier in the year. I speak briefly with the mother. She is still having major problems with her children. The mother wants me to talk to the teen, but he isn't here when I arrive. I inform dispatch to send me back if the family calls again. At any rate, I promise the mother I will drop in sometime and talk to the boy. However, I know how difficult it is for patrol officers to follow up with people. We are there one moment and gone the next. It is only by chance that we sometimes cross paths with people more than once. When that happens, it is usually for a new problem. This case is a classic example.

Then I am dispatched to take a destruction-of-property report. I meet with a woman who is upset that someone in her neighborhood keeps breaking her *Jesus Loves Me* sign that hangs from a light pole in her yard. As I enter the home, she is holding the sign in her hand. She takes me to the living room where she has a video surveillance system connected to a large-screen television. On the screen, I see my own cruiser sitting in the driveway of her home.

The woman states that she had watched unknown persons tear down the sign. She says that her neighbors are rude and only speak to her when they ask if she's going to sell her home. She says that in the winter the neighbors will plow snow from everyone's yard except hers. She says that in the summer the neighbors pull up her flowers and cut their grass only when they see her cutting hers. They do this to agitate her. She says that she can see people standing behind cars parked at her house recording license plates and talking on two-way radios. "They must have a database," she says. When I ask her about her family, she says her husband is dead and her only daughter is dying of cancer. The woman is close to 80 and lives alone. I think, "frequent flier." When I leave her home snow begins to fall as if it is mid-winter.

Not long after I leave this woman, dispatch calls for a car to respond to a pedestrian accident. The roads are now wet and slushy. We are short-staffed. All the other cruisers are tied up on calls. I answer the call, but I am across town. Just before I arrive, dispatch informs me that the victim, a black male, is likely dead. When I arrive, I meet a hysterical white male who says the victim just came out of nowhere. Before he knew it he had struck the man with his vehicle, and the man's body had smashed his windshield. It is a busy street known for prostitutes, small bars, greasy spoons, and strip joints. It is dark and some streetlights are not working. As I place the driver in the back seat of my cruiser he states, "I didn't mean to kill him. He just walked out in front of me. If he's dead I don't want to know."

I can't help but compare my bad day with the fate of the victim and the driver. The victim is dead. I wonder how his day had been prior to this. I wonder what his thoughts were and if he had any sense that today was his last day. The driver now has to live with the reality that he has taken another man's life. Regardless of what his day was like, his life is now forever changed. He will go on living with something and never make peace. As for me, my lesson is that I should never allow small things to get me down. Compared to these men, I am fortunate. I don't have any real problems. Through this experience, I am reminded of the fragility and unpredictability of life. I can only sum it up by acknowledging that sometimes it does indeed snow in April.

FIFTY-SEVEN

Violence on My Mind

I CAN'T sort out the date, time, or location of my final call. The people are all strange, frantically running around in a house. Someone has been shot or stabbed. Blood is everywhere. For some reason, I can't talk to the people and they can't talk to me. I'm not even sure they know I am here. At least they carry on as such.

I am frustrated to be somewhere and not know where I am. I am further frustrated by the fact that an invisible barrier seems to be between the people and me, although we stand in the same room. Who are these people? I can't file a report if I can't get the *who, what, when, where and how.*

Finally, I roll over in bed and look at the clock. It says 6:57 a.m. I am still sorting out the facts of that call when I realize it is a dream. My wife and I have fallen asleep with the television on. I can hear a reporter saying that seven U.S. soldiers died in the night in Iraq during something called *Operation Vigilant Resolve.* The sight of people running frantically, mixed with the sight and sound of gunfire and explosions, is presented to the American public as *Vigilant Resolve?* It feels like an extension of my dream. In the next story, the media admonishes a group of primarily white, middle-class University of Connecticut students for celebrating a basketball championship with violence. The visual is not much different than the Iraqi war scene. At that point, I have no question in my mind where these students learn to celebrate victory with violence. On the ensuing commercial break I pick up a pocket dictionary from the nightstand and find that the word *vigilant* means to avoid danger. Something is wrong with that message from the government. Later, reports of U.S. military police torturing and sexually assaulting Iraqi prisoners continues the American legacy of domination of people of color through violence.

After the commercial break, I realize that my dream is a result of the explosion of violence that I experienced on the streets the previous night.

On our first call, my partner and I are dispatched to the scene of a shooting. The body of a young black male sits limply behind the wheel of a stolen vehicle. Several bullet holes have penetrated the back window. The man has taken shots to his back and the back of his head. My partner and I begin roping off the scene as emergency medical personnel try to save the victim. As usual, a crowd of black people gather to witness the aftermath of violence, which predictably leaves another young black man dead at the hands of other black men.

The crowd likes to ask questions, but they never have any answers. "I didn't see nothin'. Yeah, I heard shots. Everybody hears shots around here. Hearing shots don't mean nothin'."

When the sound of gunfire becomes a normal part of living, the people literally live in a war zone. A murder scene becomes a public event in poor black communities. The fear of death has been replaced by an unhealthy fascination with it. People of all ages watch, desensitized. Children stop on their bikes. Carloads of people pull up as close as they can to look at the body. Mothers stroll casually by. Young black men talking on cell phones stop to watch with their pit bulls on long thick chains. The pit bull seems to be a symbol of black ghetto masculinity. Terriers, especially the pit bull, are known to be bred for fighting, thus in the ghetto they are a sign of violence. Just as the pit bull and the handgun are symbols of black ghetto masculinity, so are the bombs, guns, tanks, ships and the airplanes of war instruments of white male masculinity. Violence and masculinity combine to kill in the ghetto and in Iraq.

As I cover the neighborhood on foot, I pass several trash-filled yards of abandoned, burned-out houses that are but further symbols of violence acted out by the people in the community. A message in memory of a previous black male homicide victim is painted on the broad side of one abandoned house: *"Gone but not 4 gotten. Li'l C, a real hood nigga."*

Amid this destruction, my partner and I find a man and his son working in their well-kept yard. They heard the shots. They saw three young black men running from the area of the shooting. We transport them to the station to sit for hours and be interviewed by detectives. I complete my reports and hit the street again. Nineteen minutes later, my partner and I are dispatched to a home for shots fired. Three men have broken into a home and beat a woman and fired shots into a vehicle containing another man and woman. At the same time, dispatch reports that a dead man has been found in a liquor store parking lot a few blocks away.

My partner and I continue on to the call for shots fired. The beaten woman is transported to the hospital. Her blood is all over the porch and in every room in small house. The bullets do not hit the couple in the vehicle.

This is the stuff my nightmares are made of.

FIFTY-EIGHT

On The Seventh Day

Today, thin, almost invisible clouds make the sun appear to be shining through waxed paper.

Time is always escaping. The sun is moving further west and the wind blows strong.

I've been called to the home of a man who mourns the loss of his mother and fears for the safety of his daughter, who was threatened by some friends. He sits in a dining room chair with his back to a table and an open door. The bare wood floor beneath him has been stripped of its linoleum. He takes a long drink of beer from a 40-ounce bottle. Just then, the strong wind slams the door shut. He swallows and slams the bottle on the table and says, "That's my mother coming in. This is her home. I'm a black man. You know what I mean?" And I do. I do know what he means. About the spiritual reference to the wind and his deceased mother returning home. About being black. I know what he means.

It is time for closure. I prepare to leave him there with the old black and white pictures of his family on the walls and his electric guitar lying in the middle of the floor. Before I exit I pick up the guitar. I always wanted to play guitar.

"Do you play?" he says.

"No," I respond, gently laying the guitar down.

"I can teach you," he pleads eagerly.

I don't respond. It's time for closure. There is nothing more that we can say. Not even "bye" seems appropriate. But still, I know what he means.

Leaving his home, I drive past an old school building. It is closed now. I see three children playing on swings. My mother and I once picnicked here when I was a small child. My father never came. The tall iron slide that was made like a rocket ship is gone now. It once sat in the middle of the field now covered in dandelions.

Small trees now grow through the nets at the tennis court. Grass grows through every crack in the ground that is not covered in broken glass, and the sound of emptiness echoes for miles around. Four sturdy iron supports for basketball hoops are still firmly planted in the cement but gone are the backboards and the rims. "Trees without leaves," I think. "Trees without leaves."

The children wave and smile.

"Hi police," they always say. Sometimes they race the cruiser on foot as far as they can go. I wonder if their happiness will end when the race is done. They seem happy and I'm glad they can express it. Thinking back to my days as a child in that same park, I wonder if I was happy. I was about their same age. Where are the parents? I wonder. Where are the parents?

Not far from the park, I pass a church where prostitutes do business on the doorsteps six days a week. On the seventh day, the Christians come and the preachers preach, but the people who need them most never hear a word. I wonder what Christians and preachers do on weekdays. I am tempted to question God about the things I see, but I catch myself. There must be a reason for this, and it must not be for me to know.

At least not now. Maybe never, but that doesn't stop me from wondering why a young black mother is addicted to cocaine and leaves her three children alone while she goes "to the store." She says she left them with a friend, and when she returns, they're gone. She says one child had no pants and no shoes and socks on. When search dogs can't locate her children, the mother rolls on the ground and screams, "I can't live without my children." My instinct tells me that if she had really gone to the store, she would have taken her children. Hours later, the children are found safe. A family friend had picked them up to teach the mother a lesson when she found them wandering outside alone.

Teenagers have assumed control of the streets now. I question whether they fear authority or authority fears them. Some unspeakable thing is lost, never to be found again. It seems that it can only be resolved if God were to start the world over again. The fire next time. God gave Noah the rainbow sign.

When I was a child, it always seemed that parents outnumbered children, but now it seems the children outnumber the parents. It must have been the strength of the adults that made them seem numerically superior, just as weakness today makes them largely invisible.

A 13-year-old girl is pregnant by a 28-year-old man across the street. The girl's mother stabbed the man in the chest. "Yeah, I stabbed him. He deserves to die. He raped my child," she shouts. The family of the stabbed man fires shots into the mother's home. After the riot, the mother goes to jail, the rapist goes to the trauma room and the girl goes to get an abortion. I ask myself, "Will any of us survive the times?"

A man strikes a child on a bike with his van. The crowd orders him to stop, but he smiles a wicked smile and keeps going. He takes with him the value of human life. He leaves behind grief, tears, screams, anger, pain and injury. The child survives. There must be a God, but still I have questions.

Grown men ride bikes more often. Perhaps they are traveling back to childhood. Or maybe society has taken from them the chance to be men, a chance to work, lead and build families and communities.

People park their cars on the lawn. The respect for boundaries continues to erode.

Young men shoot dice on the back stairs of an abandoned home. They run when they see me, but I don't chase them. Why do they expect to be hunted? I would like to talk to them. I would like to know why. Why do they shoot dice there? Why do people sell dope? Why do people buy dope? Why do people use dope? They would think I'm crazy for asking. I would think they're crazy for not having an answer. They've been programmed to be statistics for the system. What percentage will die at birth? What percentage will graduate or drop out of school? What percentage will be murdered? What percentage will go to prison? How many will be unemployed or homeless? How many will marry or have children out of wedlock? How many are more likely to catch AIDS, develop cancer, diabetes or heart disease? Their biggest contribution to society is that they will fit into one negative category or another. They have been dehumanized. Reduced to numbers.

Still the hustlers push lawn mowers and carry cans of gasoline and the elders seem confined to their porches with solemn faces. Like the children on the streets, they don't have anywhere else to go.

The large brick building on the corner once was a grocery store, but today not one major grocery store remains in the poor black section of inner-city Flint. All sense of neighborhood and community is gone.

Can it ever return?

I say to myself, "The sun is moving further west and the wind blows strong. Time is always escaping. Humanity is losing daylight. Is there really a reason for everything under the sun?"

There is a God, but where are the mothers, fathers, Christians and preachers? Maybe they have all gone "to the store." They are probably wondering where the police are. They too are probably tempted to question God. Somebody's got to be responsible for saving us from ourselves, but nobody is qualified.

The sun has set now. The wind has calmed. Time is escaping. Things never change, and things will never be the same.

Epilogue

I AM working third shift alone when I am dispatched to take a domestic assault report. Nearly there, I am flagged down by the victim, an African American woman. She is frantic. She has several scratches on her face. Her bottom lip and right eye are swollen. She had escaped to a neighbor's home with her two small sons after her husband beat her in the face with his fist, body slammed her twice to the floor and smashed all the windows out of the house. She has no phone in her home.

It is nearly 3 a.m. This woman shouldn't be standing in the street, nor should her children be awake, yet the boys stand alert inside the safety of a stranger's front door. I can see their tiny faces pressed to the glass. Their fearful expressions say they are watching to see if Mommy is OK. This is the second time tonight I have been called to this address because of assaults by her husband. Both times he has fled the scene.

This time, he has threatened to kill her, and I know she believes this because she is trembling in fear. She holds her right elbow with her left hand and complains of pain in her right arm, which met the floor twice during the assault. She seems to be on stage as she stands in the middle of the street beneath the glow of a full moon and speaks of her trauma.

My own instinct as a police officer tells me this man may be capable of murder. I have seen many domestic assault cases, but not many where a man will cause his own children to be homeless. I wonder what type of man this is. I am frustrated again with trying to make sense of the senselessness. Before I can finish the thought, the woman tells me he is a drug user and currently unemployed. She is the sole support of the family. I stare at the moon for a few seconds and try to grasp the surreal quality of the moment. A gut feeling develops. I need to find this man so he does not further harm this family.

The neighbor has volunteered to drive the woman and her children to a relative's home. In a poor black section of town, where the idea of community and neighborhood has all but diminished, I am glad a neighbor is so caring. The victim states that her husband knows the address of her relative and will eventually come there looking for her. Like many domestic violence victims in this city, she gives me the sense that no matter what she does, no matter where she goes, she will not be able to escape the reach of her abusive husband. She gives me a description of his vehicle and the license plate number. She believes he might be at his parents' home just blocks from where we stand. Before leaving the woman and her children, I assure her I will do everything I can to find her husband and put him in jail. She thanks me and seems a little relieved as she loads the children into the neighbor's car.

I leave to drive to her husband's parents' address to see if I can spot his car. If it is there, I will call for backup and arrest him. I am just one block from my destination when I notice a city police cruiser behind me. Suddenly it speeds past me and the officers make a traffic stop of a vehicle driving in front of me. I am unsure why they make this stop, but I stop behind them to be sure they are safe before I continue my search.

I watch as the two familiar white officers approach each side of the vehicle. I note that the officers have not felt sufficiently threatened to broadcast the stop to dispatch. I continue to watch as they speak with the occupants of the vehicle. Both they and the occupants seem at ease as one officer casually searches the glove compartment of the car. I pull my cruiser next to them and attempt several times to establish non-verbal communication, but they don't acknowledge me. Eventually, I decide the situation is safely handled and leave to continue my search for my suspect.

I drive ahead and am making a right turn onto the street of my destination when I hear one of the officers I just left yell on the radio that he and his partner are on a traffic stop and a cruiser has just driven past them without providing backup. I then am certain the officer who is making the broadcast was indeed ignoring my attempts to communicate with them.

Dispatch reacts to his sudden broadcast by excitedly asking the cruiser in question to identify itself. Knowing dispatch is referring to me, I respond by stating that I am conducting a follow-up investigation on the domestic assault. I am thinking of the woman and children. I continue to check for the suspect's vehicle and don't find it. Then a black male sergeant orders me by radio to return to the traffic stop. However, before I can do so, the order is canceled. Apparently, because of the officer's inflammatory broadcast, several officers have now sped to assist at the stop, thinking they are in danger. As it turns out, they weren't. In fact, I later learn that they made the stop when an occupant tossed out a cigarette. They encountered no problems, and no arrests were made.

Because I am canceled, I decide to continue my investigation and check the address to which the woman and her children have moved, to ensure that her husband has not gone there. Then, I drive again to the original address of the crime to see if perhaps he has returned, which he has not. Having exhausted all possibilities to find the man, I can do nothing more. I will file the report for the woman and she will need to seek an arrest warrant for her husband with the help of a detective.

More than one hour later, I am ordered by a black sergeant to meet with him. He informs me that he is giving me an oral discipline for failing to back up the officers on the traffic stop. When I asked him if he has spoken to the other officers, he states that he has not. He admits he has not conducted an investigation, and he is not a witness to the incident, therefore, I have to wonder what information has influenced his decision.

He refers to the radio traffic of the other officer as if this is all the proof he needs that I have done something wrong. I try to explain that I did stop with these officers well before the broadcast, but this doesn't make an impact. I begin to understand what a citizen must experience in a similar situation. I began to feel trapped and suffocated.

The fact that I am black and the other officers are white weighs heavily on my mind. The fact that the sergeant is black and willing to lend more credence to the allegations of a white officer is devastating. The message is clear. "White is right and black is wrong." They are the victims and I am the suspect, and the concept of all police officers being "blue," thus equal, is not true.

By the end of my shift, I learn that my shift commander, a white male, has initiated an investigation against me, claiming that I have invited questions of cowardice and discredited my department by refusing to back up officers who are "crying for help while embarking on a potentially dangerous activity." In the world of law enforcement, these are firing words.

He never makes an attempt to speak to me, yet, if his claims about me are true, I would be a liability to both my fellow officers and the public. However, I am allowed to remain on the street even though, according to his report, I have committed "unconscionable" acts. Further, he labels me a "coward" and a "discredit." His words are cold and calculating in his rush to judge me.

The following day my patrol assignment is changed by the shift commander. I find this especially suspicious since several white officers on my shift who are being investigated for routinely abusing black citizens, (one such officer who is involved in my case) have not had their work assignments changed, and they are certainly not referred to as cowards or discredits to the department. These allegations are highlighted in various newspaper articles.

I file complaints with the local NAACP, the Department of Justice, the FBI, and the Michigan Civil Rights Department. All claim to have varying degrees of information about the abuses allegedly carried out by the white police officers.

I file my report of the incident with a new shift commander. In my report, I state that I perceive the claims made against me by my former shift commander (a white male, and friend of this new commander) to be racist.

"Don't you think this is a little inflammatory?" he asks. "You are a man of letters, a published author, a community activist. You shouldn't come down to his level. You are a bigger person than this. What good will you do? What good will it do the department? Are you sure you want to say this? Maybe you should just tear this up and take some time to think about it."

I am stunned and his words hurt me deeply. They suggest *I* am the problem.

With tears rolling down my face, I ask him, "Who's going to tell him to tear up his report?" When I get no response, I stand up and walk out.

Ultimately, the black sergeant who disciplines me is disciplined himself for his improper action without conducting an investigation. My new commander, (the one man who had the power to impact injustice) who was originally placed in charge of the investigation, removes himself from the issue when

I refuse to change my report. Additionally, not long after the event, the shift commander is removed from his command position.

I receive a three-day suspension, which I refuse. This seemingly inconsequential punishment would likely involve me losing seniority, placing me at the bottom rung of the seniority ladder, putting me first in line for layoff, if the need arises, and the cycle repeats itself. Therefore, the case goes to arbitration where it is today.

I believe every decision we make as human beings impacts on other human beings. Just how my response to racism impacts on my life and others' is still unknown. However, no matter the outcome, for me the hope for social enlightenment lies in a quote by Dr. Martin Luther King Jr. I used it to close my report to my department during my investigation: "Injustice anywhere is a threat to justice everywhere."

Commentary:

Soul of a Black Cop

A scream from the bottom, Brian Willingham's *Soul of a Black Cop* is a compelling and often unnerving documentary portrait of an urban war zone in which people endure lives of quiet despair and hopelessness, trying to survive in a mire of failing schools, bad housing, inadequate health care, joblessness, drugs, and discrimination. The perspective, that of a black cop working in his own community, is unique, poignant for its humanity and sensitivity, and honest in its depictions and reflections ("making sense of the senseless"). Few books have captured as candidly the sights, the sounds, and the rhythms, the smoldering tensions and tempers of the inner city, the day to day experiences of America's interior exiles.

Leon F. Litwack, Author
Been in the Storm So Long: The Aftermath of Slavery
Pulitzer Prize/National Book Award
A.F. & May T. Morrison Professor of American History
University of California, Berkeley

Brian Willingham's extraordinary day-by-day account of his life as a cop reminds us that behind at least one of those forbidding police badges is someone with compassion and a profound understanding of the human condition. Have you ever wondered what it would feel like to sit beside a policeman in his cruiser and follow him through the day? As we read Willingham's carefully crafted memoir, we are brought close to the scenes he describes: the beaten women, the desperate shoplifters, the crack victims, the raped children, the mentally disturbed. But there are moments which save him and us from despair: the smile of a child reminds him that "children are born happy. The world makes them sad." Willingham sees beyond the cruelties of everyday life to the deeper sickness of a society that doesn't realize its own addiction to war is reproduced in the violence on its city streets. He writes gracefully, with a generous spirit.

Howard Zinn, Author
A People's History of the United States : 1492-Present
Professor Emeritus, Boston University

I found [*Soul of a Black Cop*], written by Mr. Brian Willingham, profoundly moving in its description, compassion, and deep-felt emotion. Mr. Willingham is a patrol officer in an urban police department ravaged by budget cuts in a city faced with economic decay and the social problems that come with it. The book is a series of vignettes that describe his encounters with his fellow citizens while on patrol. The vignettes presented come alive from the direct and stark descriptions offered by Mr. Willingham. They become meaningful when he connects the job tasks to his own experiences as an African-American police officer trying to find his place in American society as a veteran, black man, father, and in the end, a compassionate human being. Mr. Willingham could easily have included lurid details that would pique the interests of many. Rather, he gives the reader the human side of every encounter and a little bit of himself in the process. He gives humanity to people and situations when most of us would blame the victim or assure ourselves that this is not our world. Yet, as Mr. Willingham so aptly demonstrates, this is our world and we cannot sweep it under the rug. He correctly, but subtly, connects the human tragedies he sees every day to larger social issues like institutional racism and social class. At first glance the vignettes seem like a catalogue of experiences, but considered a little more deeply they paint a self-portrait of a man struggling with his place in the two worlds in which he lives. On the one hand he is one of the many people he encounters everyday, but on the other hand, he is the front line for people on the other side who count on him to keep these worlds apart. This [book] is profound in its depth of experience and vivid in its emotional undercurrent.

Marc Zimmerman, Professor
Department of Health Behavior and Health Education
School of Public Health
University of Michigan, Ann Arbor

This book echoes and amplifies the messages found in Alex Kotlowitz's *There Are No Children Here: The Story of Two Boys Growing Up in the Other America*, and Geoffrey Canada's *Fist Stick Knife Gun: A Personal History of Violence in America*. Through the authors' eyes, the reader leaves with two impressions. First, despite these hellish and painful life consequences brought on in part by personal decisions and structural inequities, African-American children, youth, adults, families and seniors dare hope and dream. Second, when increasing numbers of African-Americans cease to dream, or defer the dream, death and despair become certain and familiar companions. An important book, to be read by those promoting social justice, and by those who believe that all poor people deserve their plight. I will not soon forget the powerful words and stories.

I. M. Gant
Associate Professor of Sociology
University of Michigan, Ann Arbor

Soul of a Black Cop is a diary by an empathic, sympathetic and thoughtful police officer working in the poorest areas of Flint Michigan, one of America's poorest cities, and made famous by Michael Moore. The author's portraits of the troubled people he tries to help, has to arrest, or must take to the morgue are unfailingly informative and moving.

Herbert J. Gans, Author
War Against the Poor
Robert S. Lynd Professor of Sociology
Columbia University.

Brian Willingham's *Soul of a Black Cop* poignantly brings the spirit of the inner-city to his readers, who are taken to places where most are afraid to go and feel things that many are afraid to feel. It is educational to both scholars and the general public, who will forever see inner-city life and policing in a new light.

Kenneth J. Litwin
Assistant Professor
Department of Anthropology, Sociology, Criminal Justice
University of Michigan, Flint

Soul of a Black Cop is a stimulating piece of literature that captures the essence of life in an urban community. While reading [it], I found myself visualizing the stories told by Brian Willingham, and sympathizing with the realities in which many urban children live. I was frustrated by the fact that, although filmmakers fictionalize these circumstances for entertainment, many individuals live in these predicaments with their children who are expected to succeed while being reared in in these environments. I believe anyone who has an interest in urban children should read *Soul of a Black Cop*. I believe anyone who has an interest in impacting the social conditions in urban communities should read [it]. I believe university and college professors should require those with a major in education, social work, sociology, psychology, criminal justice, or other social services concentrations to read [it]. The riveting stories told in this book will certainly help them understand the realities their clients face. Brian Willingham should be highly commended for authoring this book.

Sylvester Jones Jr.
Executive Director
Big Brothers Big Sisters of Greater Flint

Afterword
A Theological Reflection on Undeserved Suffering

Brian Willingham's *Soul of a Black Cop* speaks about the tragic lives of a forgotten people. It takes the reader into wretched places most people never go. It is hard enough for any poor person to survive in the richest nation in the world. But when one is black and female, the burden of existence becomes almost too heavy to bear. Most of the people the reader meets in this black cop's diary are poor black women and children whose husbands and fathers are no where to be found, and whose government ignores the terrible circumstances in which they are condemned to live.

As a theologian, I have to say that nothing challenges the Christian faith like the suffering of the poor. How can we say that God loves the poor when their extreme, never-ending poverty contradicts that claim? Why is God silent when women are battered and murdered and two-year old babies raped? Should we not expect divine intervention in these unspeakable situations? The prophet Habakkuk anticipated our complaint, as if his righteous rage came straight out of America's inner cities.

O Lord, how long shall I cry for help
    and you will not listen?
Or cry to you 'Violence!'
    and you will not save?
Why do you make me see wrong-doing
    and look upon trouble?
Destruction and violence are before me;
    strife and contention arise.
So the law becomes slack
    and justice never prevails.
The wicked surround the righteous—
therefore judgment comes forth perverted.
                    (Hab 1:2-4 nrsv)

No people have experienced more injustice in the U.S. than its black poor, as the Katrina Storm blatantly revealed to the world. The cries for "Help" from the roof tops of flooded homes in New Orleans' Ninth Ward should have been directed not only at their government, whose President was golfing during the tragedy, but at their God who promised to protect the needy and to defend the poor.

Like Habakkuk, Job, Jeremiah, and a host of other biblical figures, every religious person is *obligated* to complain to their God about the suffering of the innocent. Jeremiah cried out to God: "Why is my pain unceasing, my wound incurable, refusing to be healed?" (15:18) Job, a popular figure in the black community, was the classic biblical complainer. Direct and uncompromising in his rage against God, Job "cursed the day of his birth," and asked, "Why have you made me your target?" (3:1; 7:20) If Christians have any doubts about questioning God, all they have to do is turn to Jesus. His agonizing cry from the cross, "My God, my God, why have you forsaken me?" (Mk 15:34), deepened the need to question God. Questioning God protects faith's integrity, for faith can only be true when it confronts suffering as its great contradiction.

While undeserved suffering contradicts faith, it paradoxically deepens the faith it questions. Again, Habakkuk anticipated faith's struggle to sustain itself in the midst of suffering.

Though the fig tree does not blossom,
and no fruit is on the vines; though the produce of the olive tree fails and the field yields no food; . . . yet I will rejoice in the Lord; . . .
God, the Lord, is my strength; (3:17-19)

How does one rejoice surrounded by so much trouble and pain? The joy is not in the suffering but "in the Lord" whose presence is a weapon against the despair that stifles the fight against injustice.

Faith can be bad and good. Bad faith accepts suffering as God's will. Good faith fights suffering. The only way that faith can be true is for people to make it true by bearing witness to truth in and through the fight against injustice.

There is not one story or one message in the Bible but many, and they do not always say what we want them to say. The same is true about life, especially life lived on the edge of existence. When faith is carved out of resistance against the chaos in America's inner cities, it cannot be superficial but real and true. A few black churches proclaim every Sunday the ability of their faith to stand up against suffering. They sing, pray, and preach about God's liberating presence with "the least of these." Such faith makes absolutely no sense to the language of reason—for when black people leave Sunday worship, they see the same terrible reality they saw before they went. After all the shouting is over, not much is changed—except the deepening of the people's spiritual and political will to resist and not to be defeated by injustice. This is the key to faith. It doesn't remove suffering. Faith emboldens people to fight against societal injustices—promising that "we shall overcome someday," "there will be no more trouble," "we will cross the river of Jordan" and "walk in Jerusalem just like John."

Only when faith refuses to quit fighting for justice is it the hope derived from the cross of Jesus of Nazareth. Faith believes that on the other side of the cross of despair is hope in the resurrection—which is poor people rising up against the powers of injustice, declaring "no justice, no peace!" The biblical God does not promise that people will not suffer, but rather that suffering does not have the last word. God is present in the struggles of the poor, suffering with them and empowering them to fight the evil in their midst. That was the faith of Martin Luther King, Jr. and Malcolm X, and it ought to be our faith too.

-Dr. James H. Cone is Charles A Briggs
Distinguished Professor of Systematic Theology at
Union Theological Seminary, New York.
Author of God of the Oppressed

Brian Willingham lives and works as a police officer in Flint, Michigan, the city of his birth, with his wife and three children. He is the author of *Thunder Enlightening, the poetry and photography of a Black man in middle America*. Among his achievements, he received the City of Flint Human Relations Commission Police/Community Relations award and was designated a Distinguished Alumnus of Flint Central High School in the field of human rights. Recently awarded President's Volunteer Service Award.

To contact the Author visit him online:
www.soulofablackcop.com or via email:
bkwillingham1884@sbcglobal.net

810-513-1407

Printed in the United States
83103LV00001B/52-99/A